# The Pastor's Guide
# to Youth Ministry

# The Pastor's Guide to Youth Ministry

AMY JACOBER

Abingdon Press / Nashville

THE PASTOR'S GUIDE TO YOUTH MINISTRY

*Copyright © 2006 by Abingdon Press*

*This book is printed on acid-free paper.*

**Library of Congress Cataloging-in-Publication Data**

Jacober, Amy.
    The pastor's guide to youth ministry / Amy Jacober.
        p. cm.
    ISBN 0-687-49579-2 (binding: adhesive, pbk. : alk. paper)
    1. Church work with youth. I. Title.

BV4447.J25 2006
259'.23—dc22

2006001278

All scripture quotations (unless noted otherwise) are taken from the *New Revised Standard Version of the Bible,* copyright © 1989, by the Division of Christian Education of the National Council of the Churches of Christ in the United States of America. Used by permission. All rights reserved.

Scripture quotations noted NASB are taken from the *NEW AMERICAN STANDARD BIBLE®,* © Copyright 1960, 1962, 1963, 1968, 1971, 1972, 1973, 1975, 1977, 1995 by The Lockman Foundation. Used by permission. (www.Lockman.org)

06 07 08 09 10 11 12 13 14 15—10 9 8 7 6 5 4 3 2 1
MANUFACTURED IN THE UNITED STATES OF AMERICA

*I am grateful for all of the input I have received from talking with pastors all over the country. I am most grateful to Rick Bennett, a wonderful pastor and good friend who is dedicated to ministry of all ages. His insight and practical help pushed many of the ideas in this book.*

# CONTENTS

INTRODUCTION. . . . . . . . . . . . . . . . . . . . . . . . . . . . . . . . . . . .ix

CHAPTER 1: TALKING TO GOD—PRAYER . . . . . . . . . . . . . . . . .1

CHAPTER 2: WORKING FROM YOUR STRENGTHS. . . . . . . . . . . .7

CHAPTER 3: VOLUNTEERS: WHERE TO FIND THEM AND
WHAT TO DO ONCE YOU HAVE THEM. . . . . . . . . .15

CHAPTER 4: ISOLATION—GOOD FOR A RETREAT,
BAD FOR DAILY LIVING . . . . . . . . . . . . . . . . . . . .27

CHAPTER 5: IF YOU BUILD IT, THEY MAY
(OR MAY NOT) COME . . . . . . . . . . . . . . . . . . . . . .35

CHAPTER 6: YOUTH TODAY . . . . . . . . . . . . . . . . . . . . . . . . . . .47

CHAPTER 7: GO WHERE I SEND YOU—AND I AM SENDING
YOU WHERE THEY ARE . . . . . . . . . . . . . . . . . . . .57

CHAPTER 8: JUST BECAUSE YOU WERE ONE ONCE DOESN'T
MEAN YOU KNOW HOW TO TALK TO THEM NOW. . .63

CHAPTER 9: IF YOU TAKE NOTHING ELSE FROM THIS
BOOK . . . . . . . . . . . . . . . . . . . . . . . . . . . . . . . . .75

# INTRODUCTION

Long ago someone said to me that youth ministry was more like cooking with a slow cooker than with a microwave. I thought this was such a stupid phrase at the time, but with a few more years behind me I can now see some of the wisdom. While teenagers come with great energy, an endless supply of drama, and new ideas, they also come with the reality that they are still growing and developing. They are not little adults, nor should they be expected to be. Time with them is not wasted even when you do not get to witness the changes in their lives. The key concept to remember for those interested in their lives is not change; it is time. Change will come; it is inevitable. You can (and should) be intentional, but don't look to quick change as a measure of success or failure. Some of my seemingly most active youth ministry students have completely stepped away from church as adults. Some of my most problematic teenagers are now following Jesus daily and seeking ways to serve and honor God with all they do. The cooking analogy certainly has flaws but there is something to the idea that slow and steady brings the results we desire. Don't rush the process. Slow down, enjoy the ride, and join God as God works to transform the teenagers in your world.

Paul writes to the church at Corinth, reminding them that he has a specific task with them. He even talks to them as babes in Christ. They need milk before solid foods. They need to be fed spiritual truth in a way that is palatable. Teenagers need to hear about the truth of Christ and what it means to follow him daily in ways they can comprehend. More important, you need to do what you have been called to do.

Often youth pastors are notorious for wanting to save every teen. This passion gives way to the deeper understanding that *we* church professionals do not save; Jesus does. It is better to talk about growth. Pastors and youth workers want to grow their teenagers, numerically and spiritually. But even that desire does not express what working with youth is all about.

A good friend of mine says his biggest pet peeve is a toaster that doesn't toast. Translation: when you have a specific task, you should do it. In the Bible, Paul goes on to say, "What then is Apollos? And what is Paul? Servants through whom you believed, even as the Lord gave opportunity to each one. I planted, Apollos watered, but God was causing the growth. So then neither the one who plants nor the one who waters is anything, but God who causes the growth" (1 Corinthians 3:5-7 NASB). We are but fellow workers. We are not the ones who cause (and conversely who prevent) growth. Our only task is to plant or water. Do it, and do it well. I am not God, and you are not God; but you do have the blessing and privilege of being called to be a fellow worker in loving and guiding God's creation.

"I loved being in a small youth group." This is the statement I hear over and over again as I ask young adults about growing up in churches. Too often we ministers get a complex that only the big churches can really do youth ministry, or that only those with a full-time youth pastor can affect the life of a teenager. These ideas simply are not true. I asked these young adults what specifically they liked, and here are a few of their responses.

- I liked being included as an actual member of the church, not a subgroup.
- I liked having extended church family caring for me, and that is what I hope to imitate some day.
- Some of my favorite days were spent helping out in the office at church. I didn't have anywhere to go after school and the church always welcomed me. Those days led to long conversations with my pastor and the secretary while finding whatever leftovers we could in the church kitchen.
- It was cool to talk with my pastor midweek when he was still working on the sermon to see that it didn't just drop out of the sky completed.

- I'd talk with my friends in other youth groups, and, while they seemed cool and fun, they almost never got real time with their leaders to talk about life and God and stuff.
- I always felt important. My pastor would find ways for me to be a leader. I was greeting before worship while I was still in junior high and playing in the worship band by ninth grade.
- Those people are still important for my life even though I'm not in high school anymore.

These comments resulted not from my asking young people to encourage pastors looking to better minister to teens. I simply asked if any of them had been in a small youth group without a full-time youth pastor and what that was like. This wasn't written to make you feel better (though I hope it is an encouragement). It was written to let you know what real life, college-age young adults are saying.

My own early youth group years were spent in a group composed of me, Carolyn, and Billy. We had no youth pastor and yet this was the place where my journey with Christ began and grew. I loved this church. I still love this church. I loved the adults who poured into our lives. It was in this small group that I learned what it was to be a part of an intergenerational congregation. I sat next to people who were not my biological family but who loved me dearly. I also loved them. I was encouraged to find ways to serve and was valued for what I could do. I was also disciplined for the things I did wrong. I had adults not only paying attention to me, but also teaching and guiding me. I had a pastor who worked to keep us informed of what was happening in our area with camps, retreats, and concerts. While I was far from perfect as a teenager, I vividly remember the great experience I had. I am always shocked when I talk with friends or students who tell stories that are not quite so optimistic. Many teens simply go to church because their parents force them. Can you imagine what it would be like if you were able to flip the script, helping those who are forced to attend church to become actually grateful and ask to be a part of the community? Can you imagine the role you might be playing in the life of a teenager so that he or she might look back with the same fondness I related? Can you imagine what a difference you can make?

As the pastor, you are indeed the shepherd. This doesn't mean you always have to be the one right with your youth, but you do set the tone for how your entire church approaches teenagers. Are youth celebrated or told to be quiet? How judgmental is your community about what may be strange clothes and hairstyles? And what about the carpet? If it gets a stain or two, does the world come crashing down? Loud music, late nights, and disinterested looks can all be a part of adolescent life. So can great volunteers, hard workers, and vibrancy! As you look at your youth, do you see all they have to offer or all they take away? Your point of view can be the difference between a church that learns to love youth and a church that drives them away.

Working with teenagers is a lot like traveling. It can be an exciting adventure or a stressful necessity. Some people just travel better than others. It may have to do with circumstances or your own personality. While you can never predict every situation, you can go with a plan. Of course it also helps to be ready for occasions when that plan has to be adjusted. I love traveling with my best friend. She is amazingly organized and always has a plan. I, on the other hand, anticipate the last-minute changes, always assuming something will be delayed, a reservation will be lost, or someone won't show. My friend and I are always over-prepared, and always ready to be flexible. Youth ministry is much the same. It can be the greatest joy, filling you with life and energy, or it can be the most stressful, mind-zapping, anxiety-producing time of your week. Much of this book will walk through the needed preparations with the constant reminder—be flexible.

Although I can't promise that all anxiety and questions will be cleared up, I can offer travel plans. You will have to flex, you will have to adapt things to your own setting, but you don't need to go clueless. While you may have more skills and tools than you think, my job is to give you a map, a guide, and a few emergency numbers just in case.

All hope is not lost if working with teenagers is simply not your passion. Not everyone is going to be called to work with every age group in the world. As the pastor, however, it is important for you to know that the current generation of adolescents and the children coming up behind them is the largest group of people this country has ever seen. We have no shortage of teenagers, and unless things change dramatically, we will not in the foreseeable future. Seeing them as Christ sees them does not mandate you as *the* point of contact, though it may. Seeing them as Christ sees them opens you up to being authentically in relationship with them. But even if you are not the one to be their leader, you can authentically be interested in finding and supporting someone to fulfill this role.

Most of what I now know was learned through the back door. I was asked to lead, to teach, and to minister, and only after many mistakes did I begin to catch a clue that I needed some help. My first position as a youth pastor came as a result of applying at the local public high school as a substitute teacher. The woman accepting applications looked at my resume and asked if I would be interested in talking with her pastor about being a minister. I would never have applied at a church but figured I had nothing to lose by heeding what I perceived to be the Holy Spirit working through this woman. Little did I know that would change the course of my life! I worked with a pastor who loved teenagers and set me up for success. He let me dream, he let me make mistakes, and he supported me through it all. And a little secret: my full-time joy only paid $100 per week. The church was small and they didn't have a lot of financial resources; but what they lacked in cash they more than made up for in support and creativity. Your church may not even be able to afford a full-time youth pastor at all. You may be the only full-time staff person, but do not give up on the youth in your area. Pray, be supportive, be intentional, and keep your eyes open, trusting that the Lord will provide.

I remember that job interview clearly—in particular the time when I met the youth. On that first night before they offered or I accepted the position, one of the youth demanded to know how I was going to teach her about God, given that she didn't believe the Bible was a valid document. I didn't see that question coming! I took a deep breath and was humbled. I never imagined how deep teenagers could be if given the time and relationship to show it. But I shortly found out.

Humility will be your ally when entering the world of youth ministry. We all have much to learn. As adolescents continually change, so must we be willing to continue to learn. It's OK to not have it all figured out. In fact it is to your (and their) benefit to openly confess not knowing something and to work through the process of learning and discerning together.

This book offers insights, encouragement, and a few helpful hints along the way. It may also set the stage for the learning about youth ministry that you will be doing for years to come. Chapter 1 begins where all ministry should, in prayer. This includes both reminders for you to pray and a look at teaching teens to pray. Chapter 2 addresses working from your strengths. Many of us have ideas in our minds of what youth ministry should look like, but we don't have the skills that fit this picture. Realistically, there is no one way to do youth ministry, and this realization frees you to do the best job that you can do with what you do best. Chapter 3 celebrates teamwork and the issues surrounding recruiting and retaining good volunteers. Chapter 4 reminds you that you are not isolated in your love for teens. In fact, there is a great supportive community of people who feel called to this age group. Chapter 5 encourages you to incorporate your youth into the planning and programming of both youth ministry and the total life of the church. Chapter 6 offers a quick overview of the history of adolescence and, more important, some major markers in the life of youth today. Chapter 7 reminds us to be imitators of Christ by going where teens are. We cannot expect them to come to us just because we have opened the door. This chapter also looks at ways of meeting teens and partnering with parachurch organizations. Chapter 8 offers insights and tips for talking with and to teens. It covers both one-on-one conversations as well as speaking to a group of youth. Chapter 9 covers some of the nuts and bolts as well as shifts in youth ministry in the last twenty years. A sad but true reality is that youth ministry creates an awareness of some of our worst societal problems. While there is a wealth of information about youth, this chapter will give you some essential resources and hotline numbers.

As you read this book, I pray that you will be blessed to seek God's guidance in loving youth and empowered to pass that love on to others.

# CHAPTER 1

# TALKING TO GOD—PRAYER

*He is one of those kids who simply touched our lives more than we expected. His name is Michael, and he is sixteen years old. His mother left the family five or six years ago. His father is a carpenter and quite elderly; consequently he cannot work more than a few small jobs to provide for the family. Oh—and Michael has two brothers and a sister. We were on a mission trip in Africa when we met Michael. I noticed he would take a bucket from the back door of the kitchen at the end of meals. He was carrying our leftovers home so that his family would have something to eat.*

*I'm not certain if it was his smile or his personality that lit up the room, but there was no mistaking if he was present or not. He laughed! He was chatty and could play the djimbe amazingly. We spent nearly a month being blessed by getting to know this young man. It was a regular occurrence for him to ask, "Auntie Amy, can I pray . . . for you?" He always knew what projects we were doing and even learned a great deal about our lives back in the states. He is a prayer warrior. He is a young man who literally has only plastic flip-flops, and he gave, repeatedly, to us. Our experience with him was a humbling lesson and a tangible reminder that God indeed longs to hear from God's people.*

## Pray for Your Youth

It is no secret that apart from prayer, we are simply operating out of our own strength. Choosing to work with teenagers is no different than any other part of pastoring in this way. Begin with yourself, and cry out to God for your youth! They are a blessing; thank God for the youth you do have in your church. They are a responsibility; ask God to lead you in where and how you can shepherd and guide them. They are affirming; when you give you really do receive! Teenagers may not generally write nice thank-you notes; but look at their lives, see where God is at work, and know that they can affirm your calling and encourage you. I'm not saying that you need to spend hours in prayer for your teens, prostrating each day (though I wouldn't be opposed). But do include them in your regular prayer time; and if prayer isn't already a part of your everyday life, now is the time to start.

Enlist a team of others to focus on your youth. This can be one or two others or an entire Sunday school class, but choose people who you know will pray. They will become your most valuable youth workers. They may never volunteer to chaperone a retreat or to host Bible study at their house, but make no mistake, they are important. There are several ways to do this. One of my favorites is to ask a group to pray in general for the youth and for what God is doing in their lives. Then, assign an individual youth to each person. While they are to be praying for all of your teens, they will take ownership and cry out to God in particular for Christine or Charlie or ____ (insert names of your youth here).

You can also invite the church to be in prayer during special times. The week before a camp or a retreat, place the name of each youth on a 3 x 5 card. As you make the announcement reminding the church that your six youth are about to leave, ask if there are volunteers who will pray for them individually. Explain that you have cards with a different name on each one. As they take a card, they must get a note back to you within the week to send with the youth on the retreat. It's a small gesture that goes a long way. It also connects your youth with someone

2

whom they might otherwise barely know. It is neither a long-term commitment nor a difficult task, so getting volunteers should be no problem.

Below is a list of thirty-one possible prayer needs for teens. This is not an exhaustive list; feel free to change it or add to it as you need. It is just in case you aren't certain where to start. Pray each day of each month for the specific area listed. This should make it bite-sized and easy to add to your daily conversation with God. Just as the Israelites needed manna, teens need you and your prayers daily!

Pray for:

(1) the youth in your church by name

(2) friends of your teens you have met

(3) the schools your youth attend

(4) friends of your teens you have not met

(5) the families of your youth

(6) discernment and wise decision-making by your teens

(7) the teachers in your community

(8) the school administration in your community

(9) athletic coaches in your community

(10) extracurricular leaders such as band directors, dance team sponsors, and so on

(11) workers at the community center or parks and recreation centers

(12) relationships amongst teens, both friendships and dating

(13) the identity issues with which they struggle

(14) financial issues/employment

(15) God's presence during times of peer pressure

(16) abused teens, protection from harm, and for the situation to be brought to light

(17) the media: TV, radio, movies, and all of the messages sent to teens

(18) protection against drugs and alcohol

(19) parental relationships

(20) the pressure to perform, to be perfect

(21) those in your community who self-medicate with food; bulimia, anorexia, and overeating

(22) the salvation of teens

(23) attitudes not to get them in trouble

(24) teens to be able to recognize when someone is trying to help them

(25) your youth to be able to recognize the good things they have instead of always longing for more

(26) issues of poverty that impact many teenagers in the U.S. and around the world

(27) teens with disabilities and all the difficulties that they face

(28) safety in an increasingly violent world

(29) time for them to be kids, to play and laugh

(30) God to grab hold of their lives

(31) No one to look down on their youthfulness, and for them to give no reason for others to look down on them

## Pray with Your Youth

Your students can become a great force of prayer in the church. In too many settings only the elders of the church ever get to pray corporately. This kind of modeling is good and necessary, but they are not the only ones who can talk to God. Teens give three common responses when they are asked to pray. The most common is one of sheer terror—not knowing what to say, feeling stupid, and wishing they could melt right into the floor. The second is being willing but certainly not joyful about the prospect. Finally is the rare but amazing occasion of having a teenager who loves prayer and is willing to go deep with it. All three are valid but not all three are profitable. Prayer is not an occasion to show off eloquence, but neither should someone feel ashamed of the words he or she chooses. Part of your role is fostering an environment where your students can pray using their own voices, their own expressions, as they call out to the Lord.

While it may seem like stating the obvious, we all needed to be taught about prayer at some point in our past. Many teens don't actually make the connection that prayer is talking to the creator of the universe, to God almighty! They know it is praying to God; but the thought of God hearing and responding, or of this really being a conversation as though you were sitting across the table from God, is not there. Prayer for many youth is kind of an ethereal tradition. Not only should you pray with your students, but also you should teach them about prayer and how to do it.[1] This always makes me nervous. It's one thing to know how to do it, and it's another to try and teach it! Do a little research; ask your youth to do some research too. Spend some time defining prayer, seeing what Scripture has to say about prayer, both Old and New Testaments. Study the Lord's Prayer. The freedom that this brings releases the group from believing there is only one right way to pray. Gone will be the days of believing that a whispered voice with hands folded and eyes closed is the only valid way to communicate with God.

## Praying Done by Your Youth

As much as youth need to be prayed for, they need to be praying for others as well. They are just as much a part of your community as anyone else. Bring prayer requests before your students. Give them time together to pray for the rest of the church. They don't need to be sheltered from the struggles occurring in the community around them. This is also a great time to remind them of the greater Christian community throughout the world. Pray for Christians in other countries; pray for your missionaries; pray for the persecuted church. Prayer is an incredibly intimate way to communicate. This practice creates a bond within your group and more important with God and the greater Christian community throughout the world. Above is a list of thirty-one prayer suggestions. Now, create a new list with your students. You can choose themes, such as prayer for non-Christians, prayer for those struggling with war and poverty, prayer for family, whatever, but let them decide the specific item for each day. Type the prayer list up and send it home with each student. This would also be a great poster to have up in the room where you meet.

## Prayer Is Not Optional

Working from your own strength simply will not last. Your youth will also not be with you forever (though it may feel like it sometimes!). Prayer is able to connect them with other believers around the world. Foster an environment of prayer in their teen years and you will set patterns for life. May you too be encouraged and blessed as you seek the face of the Lord crying out to God!

## Note

1. There are several good books written with youth in mind in this area. A few of those are: Tony Jones, *Soul Shaper: Exploring Spirituality and Contemplative Practices in Youth Ministry* (Grand Rapids, Mich.: Zondervan, 2003); Tony Jones, *Read, Think, Pray, Live* (Colorado Springs, Colo: TH1NK, 2003); and Steve L. Case, *The Book of Uncommon Prayer: Contemplative and Celebratory Prayers and Worship Services for Youth Ministry* (Grand Rapids, Mich.: Zondervan, 2002).

# WORKING FROM YOUR STRENGTHS

*I never dreamed being a carpenter, chauffeur, painter, counselor, musician, and coach would all be a part of being a minister. I did not receive this training at any workshop, let alone at seminary. And yet this was exactly what I learned in my first year of being on staff at a church.*

*Other tasks were not so easy. There was a time when I tried really hard to wear every hat that came my way. I must say, I have learned a great deal. I now know how much paint to buy to cover the walls of a room and that I will never be a professional guitar player. I learned that I can coach softball but not soccer. I have had to learn what my limitations are, where I can learn, and most important where I am strong. Instead of spending so much energy trying to do things for which I have no skill, I have learned to refocus.*

## This Book Is for You

If you are reading this and know that, while you think ministry to youth is important, you have either (a) no skills with teens, (b) no personal interest in doing this yourself, or (c) an interest, a few skills, but no time, then this book is for you. While some people are more naturally drawn to adolescents than others, your willingness to learn how to better minister to and with them is commendable! A popular game used in youth ministry is called Two Truths and a Lie. The rules are simply that each person in the group says three things and the others in the group guess which two things are the truth and which is the lie. Youth ministry can be considered as a twist on this game. Well, actually, you will encounter many lies or misunderstandings about ministry. These misunderstandings include ideas like: all youth workers must be young and funny, only people who are really cool can work with teenagers, or teenagers just want to be entertained. In the midst of all of these lies is one basic truth: if you work from your strengths, you are exactly the person God can use in the lives of adolescents.

## Working from Your Strengths

Teenagers need adults in their lives. While parents are consistently the most important and influential people in the life of an adolescent, many other persons are also needed (including you!). Some youth are blessed with a parent, parents, or a guardian who is active and involved in their lives. This involvement varies by degrees for many. A few will be on the opposite end of the spectrum and have little to no involvement from family. What a blessing, what a privilege that you get to be a part of their lives!

One of the biggest mistakes leaders make is to try and "look the part," whatever that means! The joke in youth ministry circles is that you need a goatee or soul patch, at least one obligatory tattoo or piercing, and that once you hit forty-five, you start to bleach your hair. While all of this might be a bit of a stretch, there are reasons for these stereotypes. Youth are also smart enough to recognize the stereotypes and to know what is authentic. Be who you are and do that well! Youth will know. Being yourself also sends youth the message that God accepts you as you are and that no one can ask any more of you. This is also one of the most difficult things to do in a world driven by image and the presentation of perfection for both you and your youth.

I have tried to learn guitar for years now. In fact, I have a beautiful guitar that I got at a great price. My guitar playing, however, is reserved for

me and God alone, and not because I am seeking those wonderful intimate moments. I am banking on the notion that by the time the music
hits heaven, some magical transformation has taken place and it sounds
much better because of the sincerity of my heart. In other words, I stink.
And not just kind of. For many, the thought of a youth meeting without
a few songs at the beginning just wouldn't be a youth meeting. I had to
get over that. I tried so hard and it ended in disaster each time. One of
my youth finally asked me why I was trying so hard. She said if she was
coming for the music, she would have gone somewhere else a long time
ago! Ouch!

Work from your strengths. If you are good at sports, find ways to play
or coach with your youth. If you are good at music, teach them how to
lead. (I wish I had had that leader when I was younger!) If you are good
at art, find projects and create things together. If you are a good teacher,
find teachable moments and share on their level. The possibilities are
endless!

I'm not all that athletic but I love to play. I am always surprised how
delighted my youth are to beat me or my team. It doesn't make them
think any less of me; in fact, it often opens conversations that may never
have happened otherwise. I am not a threat; I am not their competition.
Youth get enough competition every day, at school, at home, or on the
streets. They are not looking for a peer, another person with whom to
compete. They are looking for a relationship.

While I'm not that athletic, I do have quite a few things I can do. I
took a group of girls mountain biking. I've taught students how to cook.
I've taken hikes with a group of junior highs. I've also found the people
who can help them learn what they desire to know. I've already estab-
lished that music is not my strong suit. I do, however, have several friends
who are amazing in this area. A few youth took private lessons and a few
others formed a band. After years with no music, the Lord brought youth
who could offer what I never could! They however could not have done
this without my encouragement. Don't dismiss something just because it
is not your area.

## Your Dream for Your Youth

Use your strengths in determining the strategy for your group. It comes down to the vision you cast. When you dream of youth ministry, what does it look like? How does it fit with the rest of your church? This is similar to setting the tone for your church and how they view youth. It differs in that it goes beyond; it is the intentional work of walking alongside youth and finding others to do so as well.[1] If your strength is hospitality, host your students at your house for a BBQ, game night, or weekly Bible study. I know a man who said his only skill was fixing cars. He didn't want to teach Sunday school, give his testimony, or plan any games. He fixed cars. We got to the point where I connected him with two guys who knew nothing about cars but wanted to learn. The lessons began a little roughly and there was no set curriculum. But by the end of four years of high school, those guys knew how to work on an engine, and, more important, through conversations while working, they knew about Jesus in everyday life.

## Do What You Love and Take Others with You

I WILL DO THIS

Working from your strengths takes a little practice. You actually have to acknowledge and admit that you may not be the best at everything! Then again, you do get to acknowledge and admit that you've got quite a bit to offer. Take a piece of paper and create three columns. In one column, make a list of all the things you like to do. In the second column, list all the things you do well. In the third column, list things you would like to learn. Use these lists as a guideline. If you are great at telling stories, then do it!

Begin with what you like. It's amazing how much easier it is to be motivated to do something you actually like. It is also amazing how contagious it is to be around people who are in their element! Have you ever watched a movie or seen a special and by the end of it you too wanted to know how to use a jigsaw or run a marathon? Working out of your passions, even if you are not the best, is a great way to connect with youth.

I love to run. I'm not a great runner; in fact, I ran with a group when I lived in Seattle and our motto was, "No faster than the slowest runner"! We, however, were consistent, and our group grew because we loved what we were doing and there was no pressure. A few people who really were good runners used us as a warm-up and as conversation partners. A few people who may have otherwise never exercised on their own felt comfortable enough to get out there and try. Do what you love and take others with you.

Sharing what you do well is nothing less than working together as the Body of Christ. Have you read Ephesians 4 lately? My friend Tony taught me just last summer the correct way to shoot a basketball. It changed my whole way of playing! He took what he did well and shared it. I was pretty good academically in school, and consequently I often end up tutoring. In fact, my youth group kids told a few of their friends that I could explain algebra and the next thing I knew I was tutoring the hour before youth group and meeting a few new teenagers who otherwise would never have come to church.

One of the blessings of working in community is getting to unleash the potential in others. Find out what your people do well and let them share it with others. I've learned how to decorate a cake and how to build a fence all from leaders in the group who were willing to share what they knew. While building a fence may not seem like a deep theological act, the conversations that take place while trying to get it to stand up straight are gifts from the Holy Spirit. Going through an experience with someone allows relationships to form; and when it comes time to talk about Jesus and church, we all ask the people with whom we have relationships.

Finally, share what you would like to learn. Ask your students if any of them can teach you, and if not, go learn together! One of my roles this summer is to walk through budgeting with one of my students. In exchange, she has agreed to offer a few guitar lessons. It may be that it's time for you to work a little exercise back into your life. Does anyone know how to play racquetball? No? Great, go learn together. Learn about camping or painting a mural, learn a new language or how to create a web site. Whatever you choose, invite a few youth to come with you on this new journey. If you can't think of anything you want to learn or do, just ask them. They have so much to offer if we just take the time.

## Knowing Your Limitations Is a Strength

Knowing your own limitations is also a strength. If you acknowledge that you are a terrible teacher but you are convicted that your youth need to learn the Bible, work from that strength! Instead of teaching, facilitate a discussion, recruit a better teacher, or ask your youth to take turns leading with you present as head cheerleader and greatest fan! It's amazing how God can use those weaknesses. Some of us are so talented that we leave no room for any others to shine. It is good for your youth and your leaders to see that you are not perfect, that you are not excellent at everything. It leaves space for community and the gifts of others.

## Free at Last, but Lighten Up

Working from your strengths should be a freeing experience. It releases you from trying to prove that you are good enough. I know this may be shocking, but pastors can be quite competitive. In fact, pastors are often so overwhelmed with all of the pressures that come with leading a church that when given the chance to excel, they show off in a game or become downright nasty! If you know this is in your temperament, step away from the court or field until you can play and celebrate with others. I'm not saying to throw the game or seek less than perfection in the areas where you excel, but I am saying to lighten up. You have nothing to prove. You will be admired and respected more for what you are able to pass to others than for what you can lord over others.

## Conclusion

Any aspect of youth work should flow from your strengths. Don't try to look like the group down the street if it's not your thing. Don't try to force a program or activity because that is how it has always been done. Jesus traveled around with a ragtag bunch of people teaching, laughing, eating, and sharing his life along the way. This is all that is required of you, no more and no less.

## Note

1. A great place to start is by reading *Your First Two Years in Youth Ministry: A Personal and Practical Guide to Starting Right*, by Doug Fields (Grand Rapids, Mich.: Zondervan, 2002). Whether you read this alone or with a group, it lays out several hints and tips even for those seasoned in other areas of ministry.

# Volunteers: Where to Find Them and What to Do Once You Have Them

As you know, volunteers are the lifeblood of the church, especially for youth and children's ministry. How do you find those crazy enough to hang out with undisciplined teenagers and host them at their homes, teach them Bible study, or chaperone a lock-in? How do you excite them, prepare them, and encourage them in this important endeavor?

First of all, you must remember that volunteer youth workers do not need to be the youngest, hippest, craziest, or most fun adults in the church. As a youth minister, my best youth volunteers ranged in age from twenty-two to sixty, with most of them in their forties. In fact, many of my best youth volunteers were parents themselves. The most important nonscriptural quality youth workers can possess is the memory of being teenagers themselves.

At Bon Air Church, I was blessed with an abundance of great volunteers. I would love to tell you that I had a program you could follow to find them, but I cannot. I recruited two women in our church who seemed like good people to work with. They were close friends, very strong in their faith, and moms.

*Looking at their teenagers, I realized they were good moms. They had great (but by no means perfect) kids. I could tell they were hard workers and were committed (which, sadly, most of my volunteers were not at the time).*

*Over the course of three or four months I talked to them about their kids and asked them to give me insight into our youth and the needs of our ministry. I asked them what they would do as youth workers. Eventually, after getting them thinking about youth ministry, I recruited them. It was a natural step. They already wanted to help. And then the best part . . .*

*They asked their friends. And their friends, who would have turned me down, all said yes to them. Suddenly I had gone from a couple of volunteers who were working with kids because they themselves never grew up to a bunch of parents who were strong in their faith and remembered the things they had done as teenagers. Perfect. Well, not perfect, but great.*

## Find a Partner

You already know that ministry is not a solo project. The Holy Spirit must be with you every step of the way. I would equally say ministry should not happen apart from a community (think of all the people who traveled with Jesus!). It may seem easier at the beginning to go it alone, but as time passes, the weight of the burden can be crushing. Paul may have attempted to be all things to all people but not all the time. He took traveling companions and shared the burden and the blessings. What you need is a team!

A team takes time to build and most often does not look like the image you have in your mind. To begin, recruit a partner. When first starting out, look around. Find that person who knows you well enough not only to be a support and prayer warrior on your behalf, but who can also call you out and hold you accountable. This person may have no interest in actually being in the same room with teenagers, but he or she loves you and cares about what God is calling you to do. This person can be and will be key to your youth ministry if you allow it! In the beginning pray for (1) God to give you a burden and heart for ministry with adolescents, (2) God to begin working in the hearts of teenagers in your community,

(3) God to make clear a vision of where to begin or how to continue right where you are, (4) God to open your eyes to other leaders, no matter how unlikely they may seem in the eyes of the world, and (5) God to draw those leaders to you to share in the vision and to be supportive. If only prayer were all it took!

Volunteers show up in the most unlikely of places. I don't know who said it first but I have heard it most from Chap Clark, "Health breeds health." If you have that one person in your corner praying for you and the need for youth ministry in your church, you are already on your way to a healthier situation. Other people love to be around healthy people.

The very first thing to do: ask your youth (or a youth) if they could name one person in the church they would like to know more, who would it be? This is the person with whom to start! Ask this person if he or she would be willing to share his or her story with your youth group. Be very up-front with him or her (no one likes to be cornered after the fact!). Approach this individual personally, saying that the youth have pointed him out as someone they would like to know more. While you are currently only asking for him to share his story, would he prayerfully consider the experience and see if God is leading him to join in not only sharing his story but a season of his life with the group? Did you catch this? It is not the pathetic beg from the front of the church pleading that someone, *anyone* sit with the youth group during the Sunday school hour! It is a no-pressure invitation that allows a person to get to know a few youth whether it works out long-term or not. Even if it is just a one-time thing, you are building connections within the church. It can (and often does) turn into a new leader that you would have missed otherwise. Don't think that just because you asked your youth once, that things have not changed. Every six months or so, ask again. New people in your church or new circumstances in our world can bring about volunteers perhaps not noticed in the past. Several years ago when the movie *Pearl Harbor* was released, my home church hosted an event where the youth group and seniors of the church went to the movie together and then sat down for a lunch where teenagers got to hear the stories of those who lived through that time, including several who had been in Hawaii. New relationships were forged and some of those seniors have become the biggest advocates of youth ministry after meeting and getting to know some of their youth.

## Network

While you may think active recruiting is a God-given gift offered only to an exclusive few, it is a skill. Learn to open your mouth and talk about what you are doing. Make contacts in the community. If you live near a university, college (even community college), or community center, or if you know of any professional Christian associations, build a relationship with those who are teaching or in ministry at those locations. Many people would love to serve where there is a real need but simply don't know where to begin looking. If you make it known that your church not only has a need but that those who come will be valued and able to serve, you may just open up a whole new area of ministry.

**A word of caution: while these places can be a wonderful resource and a great way to build relationships in the community, DO NOT promise that each and every person who is interested will definitely be serving directly with teenagers. Be certain to meet with the person, have an application, ideally do a background check (if you make this standard for everyone it eases the awkwardness), and get to know him or her. While the need for workers is great, the responsibility to keep your youth safe is greater.**

## Recruit for Specific Needs

Leaders can also come in based around a need. Some of my most faithful leaders never once taught or led any kind of group activity. They were, however, faithful in prayer, in carpooling, in providing snacks, in creating flyers, in editing videos, in collecting money for camp, in tutoring, in just being present, in cleaning up the youth room, in providing supplies, the list goes on and on! I had to get over my pride and learn to make the needs known without manipulating or making others feel guilty. Talk out of the overflow of experience of what you are trying to do. If you want to have a service project day, let that come up in conversation as you seek service projects. If you are having a hard time leading games, teaching a lesson and trying to clean up, say so! You'd be amazed at those who will step forward to clean up on Wednesday nights as a "volunteer" once they realize it does not entail being the main speaker.

## Recruiting Volunteers Who Do Not Want to Be THE LEADER

A few creative ways to get around volunteers who don't want to be *the* leader are as follows:

(1) Invite volunteers to share stories about their relationship with Christ. This sharing can give speakers experience in public speaking on a topic that is intimately known to them. You may want to meet with them to encourage them and be certain they will give a coherent, non-rambling talk. Give a time limit.

(2) Assign lessons to your youth for them to facilitate. Let them know that one of your adult volunteers will be present but not necessarily the teacher. Be certain your adult volunteers either read the lesson or know what passage will be covered so that they are prepared to jump into the conversation, but it takes the pressure off them as *the* teacher.

(3) Pair up your volunteers for team teaching. This can be done either where each teaches part of the lesson or where they alternate weeks. Both will be present each time but not solely responsible.

(4) Recruit some seasoned leaders from other areas within the church to offer to mentor your new youth leader. You can have the best curriculum in the world and still feel inadequate. A real-life, praying mentor can be just the encouragement and guidance needed.

## Look for Volunteers of All Ages

Do *not* let age be a barrier. It is a blessing to have a young, college-aged leader who loves to bring on the wild, crazy games and activities that so many of us associate as the crux of youth ministry. That said, they can often be more trouble then they are worth. (See more about this later in the book.) Be willing to broaden your horizons of what a youth volunteer looks like—college-age to elderly, single, married, widowed, with kids or without.

> Age is often a barrier to those we picture for ministry but it is not the only one. What other barriers do you keep up? Education, gender, and ethnicity may be just a few. Pray that God removes the blinders from your eyes, allowing you to see others as God does and to see leaders in the most unlikely of places.

## Loving Them Doesn't Mean You Like Them All the Time

You may not always like everyone on your team but you gotta love them! The reality is that at some point in time just about everyone can get on your nerves, whether it is for not following through on something, asking too many questions, being the perpetual complainer, or simply always insisting on their own way. (Believe it or not, every once in awhile, you too will get on the nerves of someone else!) You, me, and all of the adults involved have got to get over this. Rene Rochester has a great way of looking at this. She says, "To work together effectively, we must be willing to relinquish our selfish ambitions for the betterment of the team. . . . On occasion when competing athletically, my focus would be altered because of friction with a teammate. However, something would happen the moment I would step into my uniform. . . . We were held together by the common interest, to run with excellence."[1] As workers with youth, we are held together by our common interest. This must take precedence over any personal individual issues you may have among your leadership.

## Build Common Interest

How do we build our common interest? In the ideal world (as in that one before the Fall where pride and personality clashes were nonexistent), our common interest would be in Christ. As we actually live in a sinful and broken world, we must be more intentional to spell this out. This, in itself, helps build a common interest. While you probably have some pretty good ideas of what you would like the ministry at your church to look like, your small group of leaders may as well. Have a dinner dreaming and planning session. This does not need to be anything fancy (make it potluck if you are on a budget), but spend time together in fellowship around a common goal. The team who plays well together, works well together. At this dinner have two goals: (1) to get to know at least three things about each leader that you did not know before, and (2) to create a one- or two-sentence description of what you are wanting for this ministry. Different traditions have different perspectives and it is important that you know your tradition (denomination) and community and allow your focus to spring from this. It will most likely be some combination of loving and growing adolescents in the Christian faith while sharing Jesus and inviting in those who do not already follow him. Whatever you decide, be certain that the group wrestles with this as you create a team atmosphere and community. Once in awhile, you will have someone who just does not fit.

I have had leaders who on paper seemed perfect but who simply did not share the vision of the team. One was educated, a leader in the church, knew the Bible well, was punctual, and was available. He was also pushy and refused to work where there was need. Rather, he insisted on working only with those whom he chose and felt youth leader team meetings were beneath him. At great risk to what I thought was my position, I asked him to step away from youth ministry for a season to see if this was really a team with which he wanted to serve. Within a few weeks,

> Can you think of a time when pruning really helped a ministry? What are the possible negative impacts this same action can have?

I had three people step forward to volunteer, all of whom said they wanted to work with adolescents but just couldn't as long as that particular man was involved. Pruning really can bring growth!

## Building Your Team

Just as much as any of your students, volunteers long for community, a place to belong as well. Be certain that you not only do the dreaming and planning dinner but that you continue to build relationships with and provide opportunities for further relationship building within the group. This can be simple times of fellowship before meetings or intentional nights out together. One friend of mine takes his leaders on a retreat every year—three days and two nights. At this retreat the rules are that only during designated prayer times do they talk about the youth. Other than those designated times, they relax, pray for one another, play a few board games, get to know one another, and truly retreat as opposed to wrestling with three days of chaotic planning. They have learned how to be around one another and authentically care for one another.

## Now That You Have Them, What Do You Do?

Now that you have a few volunteers, what do you do with them? There are many training opportunities all over the country. Some are extensive and can be a little on the pricey side, while others are shorter and more accessible financially. Chances are your denomination has a training program of some sort for youth ministry. This is the place I would begin, if for no other reason than to meet other youth workers (paid and volunteer) from within or at least near your community. You may want to brainstorm the kind of training you think the group would need as well as ask them the kind of training they desire. If they are looking for how to better put together a lesson, invite a local teacher to give training. If there is concern over sensitive issues such as abuse reporting or other legal issues, contact your local police department and request a speaker. The options are only as limited as your team's creativity!

Training for youth ministry happens all of the time. You may have to drive an hour or so, or it might be just down the street. These are great places to network! Look for all of the fliers that you normally toss in the trash. Youth Specialties offers *The Core*, Urban Youth Workers offers *Reload*, Group offers *Group Magazine Live*, and Saddleback Church offers the *Purpose Driven Youth Ministry Conference*. Not only do you get great information, but you meet others who have a heart for teenagers. They are volunteers, full-time and part-time workers, pastors, and administrative support. Just like your own volunteers, they will appear as the most unlikely of people. Once you are in the loop, you will learn of these events, but breaking in can be difficult if you do not know where to look. The following are web links to some of the larger and better-known training events.

National Youth Workers Convention—This is held three times around the country every autumn. It is five days long and the largest event of its kind.
www.youthspecialties.com

The Core—This is a one-day training offered around the country by Youth Specialties.
www.youthspecialties.com

The Urban Youth Workers Institute—UYWI offers a three-day conference in the spring and several one-day conferences around the country.
www.uywi.com

Purpose Driven Youth Ministry Conference—Doug Fields and others offer a time of training for experienced and inexperienced youth workers.
www.purposedriven.com/youth

Group Magazine Live—A one-day training event for just about anyone interested in youth.
www.groupmag.com/gml

## Volunteer Appreciation

It is amazing to look through Scripture and to realize that God must just love a party. God's followers are often seen in celebration. Celebrations help us remember, affirm, encourage, and rejuvenate. Be certain to take care of your volunteers with this same thought in mind. Volunteer appreciation can take many forms, the first and foremost of which is a commitment on your part to be praying for them on a regular basis throughout the year. Get your youth involved in ways to let the volunteers know they are appreciated. Your youth can send notes or a card to their workplaces, sneak to their houses and wash their cars, or offer a token of appreciation like movie tickets or a gift card to a restaurant, encouraging them to take some time for themselves and their own families—you get the idea.

While it is helpful and important to remind workers throughout the year how much they are valued, end your year with some manner of celebration! Throw a volunteer appreciation dinner and have your students cook, serve, and clean up! If you don't have the domestic dinner party gift, invite the group over, order pizza, and ask at least one youth who you know has been impacted by that leader to say so.

It is great for you to be encouraging; it is transformational for leaders to learn that they really matter to youth. A fun benefit to times of volunteer appreciation is that others take notice. People become more willing to step up if they know they will be appreciated. By celebrating those who have been faithful, retention is higher and you just may inadvertently be recruiting!

## The Risk of Burnout

Appreciation covers a multitude of struggles. There is, however, still the risk of burnout. We live in a busy, fast-paced world. Even those in more rural areas find themselves rushing from work to soccer to a meeting at the school while trying to finish evening chores, make dinner, look over homework, and get some sleep in time to start the whole process over. Add into the mix being a volunteer in youth ministry, and there are just not enough hours in the day. Be certain that when recruiting and shaping the duties for each volunteer that you are creating jobs that do not require a cape or any powers of flight or time suspension. Princeton Theological Seminary has done some research on the area of burnout through its Youth Ministry Institute. The following web address can offer some helpful insight into preventing this common problem for workers: http://www.ptsem.edu/iym/research/bridges/.

Even those with the best of intentions may not be very good at setting boundaries. While their hearts and mouths may say yes, you may find that three months into the year they are so overwhelmed that quitting seems to be the only viable option. When you begin the recruiting process, choose a set beginning time and a set ending time. Some churches choose to do this based on a one-year commitment (often coinciding with the school calendar). Others ask for a school-year commitment and a separate summer commitment. Never assume, even for the most involved of leaders, that they will continue indefinitely. As the end of your designated time approaches, meet with each leader. In this meeting offer feedback of what they have done well and where you can see a need for growth, ask for their feedback, and then once again, give the option of either remaining a leader or stepping away. Some people will never begin as a volunteer in youth ministry if they see it as a life sentence. If, however, you make it clear that it is for one year, your chances of a person saying yes increase. When you give an out at the end of the year, you honor that individual. Word travels quickly. Eliminating a situation where volunteers feel guilty for stepping away (not to mention the potential burnout if you manipulate them into staying) will help your ministry in the long run.

Volunteers make up the majority of youth workers in this country, and in the world for that matter! There is something amazing about watching the way God transforms a seemingly misfit bunch of people into a community focused on Kingdom work. The web offers many great resources to help in this process. Two resources worth mentioning are www.ileadyouth .com and Church Volunteer Central. The first is an ever-changing site with information ranging from games and logistics to curriculum and spiritual health. The second one is from a group called Church Volunteer Central, which looks at volunteers in all age groups. While this book is about youth ministry in particular, the information on this web site is priceless. See: https://shop.grouppublishing.com/cvc/

The fields are ripe and the workers are few. While it can seem discouraging when you are small, by no means does God view you as insignificant. Recruit, train, and celebrate the same whether you have two volunteers or twenty.

## Note

1. Rene Rochester, *Positioned for the Exchange: Who Will Impact the Next Generation?* (Enumclaw, Wash.: WinePress Publishing, 2002), 56-57.

# Isolation—Good for a Retreat, Bad for Daily Living

*One of the earliest gifts God gave me in ministry was to work with a wonderful pastor. He was the perfect balance of supportive and hands-off. He let me do what I thought best without micromanaging. Sometimes I did well and he was my biggest cheerleader. Sometimes I failed miserably and he was also the first to say that was all right, that next time it would be better. He was also deliberate in connecting me with others interested in adolescents. He encouraged me to attend trainings and local prayer meetings. Many of my early mistakes were made because I was trying to do it all on my own. It wasn't that I was an egomaniac; I simply didn't want to bother anyone else. I didn't want to be that person always asking for help. What I learned is that more people had to help clean up after my mistakes than would have been needed from the beginning. Not to mention that I was denying some wonderful people the blessing of serving God by working with youth.*

*Another issue for those committed to adolescents is the misunderstanding of others around you. There will always be people who wonder why so much time and so many resources are being given to a group of people who do not even serve on the building committee or the stewardship committee. Anyone called to youth at some point has to come to the realization that he or she will just have to be misunderstood by some people. There are worse things in the world. There are also thousands of others who share your heart and it is important to seek these people out. Support and community are required to make it for the long haul.*

## Needing Resources Helps You Network

Healthy youth ministry cannot be done in isolation. Youth ministry lends itself to networking. Many youth workers began doing camps in the summers and have ended up all over the country. We have grown up and moved away, though many of those friendships have remained intact. A natural result of youth ministry is that those youth grow up, they go off to school or get a job and become responsible productive adults. A few of them will even become lifelong friends.

There is a network beyond your church walls. Getting leaders and your youth connected is not only helpful, but essential. Even the strongest and healthiest of groups can feel the strain if they only see one another. It is good to know of others following Christ in your neighborhood, across the street, and around the world.

You are not alone! In fact, not even your team at church is alone. There is a great cloud of witnesses gathered who are called to minister to and with teenagers. Granted, some of your friends may not sense the same desire to intentionally pour themselves into their teenagers' lives, but you are not alone. Find others in your area whose hearts break for teenagers. Ask questions. Seek support. Find some people with whom you can pray. I was talking with some friends this weekend about youth ministry and urban youth ministry in particular. We know one another. We network. We don't have the luxury of becoming an island because none of us has the resources to go it alone. While the lack of resources can be a burden, we see it as a gift. It is a gift that keeps us linked and in support of one another long after we may have walked away. Ask your peers and the people in your life, both personal and professional, to dream with you about what may take place for the teenagers in your area. If you can't find anyone right away, check around for a few of the youth pastors who can encourage you on this journey. Not to mention, they'll be able to offer those precious practical tips! Good youth ministry is never being afraid to borrow from others!

## Finding Help

So where do you find those people? Always begin locally. Do you know the pastor down the street? Does that congregation have a youth group? I am always amazed at how isolated we become as if we are afraid to talk with other believers. It will help if, when you contact that pastor down the street, you offer assurance that you are not trying to steal church members or teenagers! I know it might surprise you but some people actually get a little territorial! Try contacting your association, presbytery, or conference to ask about youth leadership networks in your area. In fact, look to your denomination first! If none of these provide any help, get in touch with Youth Specialties, Group, Urban Youth Workers, ILeadYouth.com, or Leadership Network to ask about other leaders in your area.

Events are also a great way to connect with others. Check out what is happening near you. Water parks, amusement parks, and other major venues often have a Christian youth day. If you don't get the promotional materials, chances are your denominational office does. Invite that church down the street . . . they just might be wishing someone was helping them out as well. There are also plenty of one-day or weekend-long conferences for your youth.[1] These conferences are a great idea as they provide a common experience for the entire group along with the encouragement of being with an extended group of believers.

## What Does the Healthy Youth Group Look Like?

Many tools can be used to measure a healthy youth ministry. It should be clear by now that your youth ministry must be grounded in prayer, your leaders must be supported and receive ongoing training, and your youth need connection to a broader Christian community.[2] So now what? That all sounds great but what exactly does a healthy youth ministry look like? Take a look at the list below. Do you agree? Disagree? If you were going to rewrite it, what would you eliminate/include? In fact, gather your team and try writing your own. Compare it to what is written here and come up with your master list.

## Top Ten Signs of a Healthy Youth Group

(10) Your teens are not embarrassed to invite their friends.

(9) You know not only the names of your youth but something about each one.

(8) Your students know they are at church and not at an after-school program or community center.

(7) Other adults in the church know the names of your students and pray for them.

(6) Your church cares more for teenagers than they care about the carpet.

(5) Your group is loving and friendly to others.

(4) Your group shows a change in its thinking, attitudes, and behaviors that reflects time with God and in the Bible.

(3) Your house or office has been "decorated" at least once in the past twelve months.

(2) You and your leaders are more refreshed than drained.

(1) Your youth grow up to be lifelong followers of Christ.

# The "So What?" for Each of These Signs

(10) Your teens are not embarrassed to invite their friends.

We've all seen the best of intentions that just don't work. Some places want to have a youth ministry and just miss the mark. Their youth are embarrassed to bring anyone new around. Be authentic and, regardless of how hip or not hip you think you are, your students will love your place in their lives and want to share that with others.

(9) You know not only the names of your youth but something about each one.

Everyone likes to be known. Teenagers are not the exception. In fact, perhaps more than at any other time in life, teens are self-focused and view themselves through others as through a sort of looking glass. Ask what they like to do in their free time, ask what subject in school they like, or what kind of music they like; just ask something that shows that you are interested in knowing them as individuals and not just as a part of the youth group.

(8) Your students know they are at church and not at an after-school program or community center.

The world is a busy place. We do not have a shortage of activities to fill the hours of the day for any teenager. While church can cover a host of activities, do not neglect that what you have to offer is indeed different from any other youth organization. There will be other tutors, other coaches, and other advocates, but you are their pastor, charged with their spiritual guidance and nurturance as they grow in the Lord.

(7) Other adults in the church know the names of your students and pray for them.

Too often the only adults in the church to know teens are the direct volunteers. While this is natural, these volunteers are only a tiny portion of the greater community, and any person is only a youth for a very short period of time. Upon graduation, youth are more likely to continue at a church if they have connections that have moved beyond the youth group.

(6) Your church cares more for teenagers than they care about the carpet.

Any time you have a group of people, especially a group of teenagers, there is always potential for something to be spilled, broken, or torn. I am not advocating trashing your building, but accidents do happen. Keep in perspective that buildings and carpets were made for people and not people for them. You may be the one who needs to vocalize this point of view but it will save many headaches if you take a clear stance from the beginning.

(5) Your group is loving and friendly to others.

A youth group is not meant to be an exclusive club. The blessing of a small group is that you really get to know one another and speak into one another's lives. The struggle is that even if one new person comes, the group dynamics shift. It will be up to the leadership to keep this at the forefront of thought. Be certain that you treat others as Christ would, whether someone is visiting your group or your group is seeing people out at conferences or around town.

(4) Your group shows a change in its thinking, attitudes, and behaviors that reflects time with God and in the Bible.

This one takes time but it can be fostered weekly. Teach a lesson and the next week ask them what they remember. How could they apply what they learned? How did they apply what they learned? Be intentional about encouraging time with the Lord and helping your youth read the Bible for themselves. Look for ways their lives are reflecting this, and challenge the ways in which you see them running counter to what you have been studying. This is a fine balance, being able to condemn the sin and not your teen, as you want to protect the relationships God has placed in your care.

(3) Your house or office has been "decorated" at least once in the past twelve months.

Sounds crazy but one of the ways youth let you know that you are loved is to cover your house in toilet paper, fill your office with balloons, decorate your car with shoe polish, or a whole other host of messy but not destructive activities. This really does mean that you are liked and appreciated! Teens don't invite adults into their worlds lightly. If you have been asked to a birthday party or family BBQ, this is a strong gesture. Know that they are still developing the tools of how to express appreciation and accept these highest of compliments as gifts from the Lord.

(2) You and your leaders are more refreshed than drained.

Being with youth, when it is right, gives energy rather than draining it. This is not to be mistaken with never being tired. They will wear you out, but your heart and soul should not feel burned out. Be certain first of all that your own spiritual life is in order. Be intentional about Sabbath. If you know this is covered, consider why or how what you are doing is refreshing or draining for the leadership. Youth need adults, but they need healthy adults who want to be in their lives, not those who are volunteering by default or begrudgingly. Talk as a leadership team and regularly evaluate if what you are doing is honoring God, meeting the needs of your youth, and keeping your leaders refreshed.

(1) Your youth grow up to be lifelong followers of Christ.

While easily the most significant and important of all the indicators of a healthy ministry, this is also the most difficult. It does not even show until ten or more years after your teens have left the youth group. As much as youth ministry is about teenagers, it is really about growing individuals to passionately follow Jesus into adulthood and for the rest of their lives. Keep this goal in mind, knowing that the changing and developing lives of teenagers can only truly be measured in retrospect.

## Healthy Overflow

I have been a part of both very healthy and very unhealthy youth ministries. Often, these are simply a microcosm of what is occurring in the church as a whole. Tend your own soul; take care of yourself. This is the first step in a healthy ministry. The next is to keep your team healthy. Encourage them, empower them, support them, and, most important, pray for them. The final step is work with youth. This is to come out of the overflow of what the Lord is doing in your life and in the life of the community where you serve. Health breeds health.

## Notes

1. Check with your denomination first, but possible conferences include Student Life, Youth for Christ-DCLA, Acquire the Fire, Youth Leadership Institute from Azusa Pacific University, and the list goes on and on.

2. *The Godbearing Life* by Kenda Creasy Dean and Ron Foster is a good book for either individual growth or to be read as a youth ministry team (Kenda Creasy Dean and Ron Foster, *The Godbearing Life: The Art of Soul Tending for Youth Ministry* [Nashville: Upper Room, 1998].

# IF YOU BUILD IT, THEY MAY (OR MAY NOT) COME

*I always make it a habit to ask a few teenagers to help me lead our youth ministry. We meet together and plan together. I mentor them and let them see how ministry looks from the inside. You may not call them a youth council in a formal sense, but they are youth leaders.*

*Putting youth in charge of ministry was revolutionary to my own work. Too often I, as with many in our church, did not allow youth to do more than bring some friends, lead a song or two, or make an announcement. I did not think teenagers had the capacity to lead in ministry. It has been revolutionary for me to understand what the early church realized quickly, that the apostles could not run a church on their own and needed to designate others to help. Throughout church history, we have had non-paid leaders doing most of the work of the church. It may be that even the disciples were not much older than many of the youth in our churches. Also, I realize that my teenagers are in leadership positions in their schools, from student council to clubs and other extracurricular activities.*

*So, why can't they be in charge of their own ministry, under the leadership of me and church volunteers? What if I became an equipper and allowed them to plan the ministry and do the bulk of it? Seeing youth as partners frees me to enjoy my ministry with them more. This way youth and youth leaders don't just blindly follow me as their pastor. Rather, together we follow Jesus.*

## Planning for Success

One great fear of anyone working with adolescents is planning, pouring time, energy, and money into an event and then sitting—alone—wondering what went wrong. Relax, there are ways to prevent this from being your experience. It is true that teenagers love a great event—who wouldn't? That said, if you do not have a relationship with any teenagers in your church or community, don't bother wasting your resources.

The special events side is what most people think of first when they think of your ministry. For many people, it is what they think the entirety of youth ministry is. Although I disagree with this thinking strongly, I cannot deny that it is an often-important part of what we do. Programming includes camp, retreats, concerts, or nights out. Programming, however, also includes more regular times together like Sunday school, small groups, and even confirmation.

A caution before you spend a lot of time and money seeing what everyone else is doing. First of all, you have the greatest resources for planning and programming right at your fingertips: your youth. The rest of this chapter is about involving them. This does not mean that you have no role or responsibility in this. It is good to learn from others, to seek counsel and help. It is not good to try and replicate exactly what others are doing.

John Drane offers a good perspective on this in *The McDonaldization of the Church: Consumer Culture and the Church's Future* (Macon, Ga.: Smyth & Helwys Publishing, 2001). Although Drane's book is not directed expressly to youth ministry, it certainly applies. Drane takes the sociological theory developed by George Ritzer and applies it to the church. He discusses four major areas related to rationality or the assurance of a smooth operation. **The first element is efficiency**. This means that we move from loosely organized movements to highly structured organizations in our attempt to become as efficient as possible. Eventually we forget why we did something in the first place and it simply becomes the tradition. It is the norm not because it is thoughtfully considered, but because it is what is.

**The second element is calculability.** This has to do with size and quantity—the more the better. The problem is, we tend to equate quality with quantity. Step away from measuring by sheer numbers or being able to quantify each element. More youth activities does not equate with better, it equates with more. If this happens naturally, great, but if it is simply keeping busy with little to no substance, you are really just making yourself and your students weary.

**Predictability is the third element.** It looks at what is familiar and comfortable. What book, what program, what new approach are going to transform what is happening where you are because they worked somewhere else? Just because one program works predictably for you does not mean it will work for me at all. It leaves little room for surprises or creativity. All over the world, we are told subtly and not so subtly that doing youth ministry means looking like all the others. There are of course elements common to all, but find what works for you and your group. Learn from others but know that you are the expert for your particular community and church.

**The final element is control.** We as leaders have been socialized to believe we are in control of spirituality, the program, the altar call, and a whole host of other things when it comes to the church. After all, we are the ones who are called and will be held accountable before God one day. We have been blessed with training and have been given authority by our communities. Most of us have even been taught that being spiritual looks a certain way. There are criticisms and benefits to the entire proposal. Is it really so terrible if the music is off-key or if the opening game doesn't go as smoothly as if you had led it? Rejecting the notions that you must be in control and that it must be perfect frees you up to be more fully present with your youth and not be a professional putting on a show. For the purposes of this book, know that a pre-packaged adult-centered program will not only drain you of time and energy, but also deny the gifting, brilliance, and energy that your youth naturally bring.

I saw a commercial in England this winter recruiting school teachers. The campaign had several different commercials but they all went something like this: "If you are looking for stimulating conversation, energy at work, questions and interest in a project, a way to stay young, and an ever-changing environment, we have the job for you." They nailed it. Youth will disagree, make you laugh, talk back, be interested, express confusion, and offer a whole host of other unpredictable, inefficient ways of relating. They hate to be controlled and can tell when they are being patronized or offered consolation prizes. They are the opposite of efficiency, calculability, predictability, and control. Let them be who they are in all of their unpredictability. Teach them to be responsible with their own faith as you invite them to plan and program inefficiently.

## Beginning at the Beginning

So where do you begin? Well, at the beginning. Like any relationship, time together is the most important. This doesn't need to be completely structured and planned by you right from the start. Invite your youth to dinner. Make it informal and low-key with no agenda apart from just getting to know one another. Don't worry if you are nervous! This is normal and chances are they are too. Getting to know your youth and allowing them to get to know you apart from being up front on Sundays is key. Ask about their day; ask about school or extracurricular activities. Ask what things they love and what things they hate. Look for places to connect. You may not be excited about NASCAR or the latest fashion trends, about video games or hip hop, but if they are, listen. Let them teach you! You might be surprised to find a new hobby, a new area of interest. You won't love everything they do, but you can learn to appreciate new things. For example, I'll never be a skater; but I have learned from those in the skating community. Skating is not blading and does not share its ideology. If you're scratching your head wondering just what all of this is, spend some time with your youth. Skating and blading have their own subcultures that speak languages missed by most adults. By no means are these the only two—hip hop, pop, dance, soccer—the possibilities are endless. Whether you are in a city or a suburban or rural area, there are local interests that speak volumes if you are willing to listen.

Dinner's over. Now what? If you already have some relationship or have skills in conversation, feel free to sit around and talk. Conversation is such a lost art for so many. To sit around and actually pay attention to one another and to talk are almost unheard of. For some of your youth, this will be awkward and new. Yet they do it all of the time with one another. They go to the mall and sit in the food court or wander around for hours. They gather at some spot in town, at the drive-in or the parking lot of the grocery store, and just hang out, for hours, doing nothing. The difference is that teenagers do not often just hang out with adults. If the idea of sitting around and staring at one another and having nothing to say is terrifying; play a few games. Play charades or cards or a boardgame. Just play! Getting to laugh together is an amazing gift. Especially when our lives are so busy and time is precious, it can be hard to see the value in spending time together without a purpose, without accomplishing something. Even Jesus spent time with his followers. He went to dinner. He went out on a boat. He slowed down and talked. Playing games gives a common activity around which you can focus but leaves space for conversations. It removes that space where silence can grow and take over. This also allows a safe space to get to know things about one another that simply would not come up in a structured Bible study. One dinner will not be enough, but it is a start!

## The Place of Formal Study

As great as it is to get to know and spend time with teenagers, there is a time and place for formal study. You may be a part of a tradition with a denominational publishing house. I encourage using this curriculum for at least one meeting during the week. Denominational curriculums offer theological perspectives and education that cannot be found elsewhere. They are also written by professionals who have taken the time to be certain that the theology is sound and the methodology is geared to specific groups. Dated denominational curriculum can be priceless to leaders who may otherwise be overwhelmed with the responsibility. (Dated curriculum means that there is a lesson written for every week with corresponding dates. In other words, the lessons go along with the church calendar and often take into account the season and major events like Christmas.) You may also choose undated curriculum. Undated curriculum offers lessons typically in ten-week, thirteen-week, or even year-long varieties. The difference is that they are not tied to the date in which you are beginning to use them. Major principles are covered, but you may look at the resurrection in November and the birth of Jesus in the spring. If you do not have a denominational publishing house, don't give up now! Some people are comfortable and competent in writing their own lessons. If this is not you or you don't have time to invest in this weekly, other options are available. There are many excellent resources. It may take a little time and research. Check out the following web sites for potential curriculum. Order samples and make your choices.

www.augsburgfortress.org

www.Cokesbury.com

www.cookministries.com

www.davidccook.com

www.grouppublishing.com

www.helwys.com

www.ILeadYouth.com

www.lifeway.com

www.standardpub.com

www.studentlife.net

www.thomasnelson.com

www.tyndale.com

www.upperroom.org

www.urbanministries.com

http://www.gbod.org/youngpeople

www.zondervan.com

Choosing a curriculum is the first step. You may even want to invite your youth to look over some of these with you. Reality is we are not all naturally gifted at teaching. Even the best of teachers may not be gifted at talking with or teaching teenagers. Use the curriculum but involve your students. Have one or two look over the lesson the previous week and offer the opportunity to facilitate the lesson. The more ownership they have, the better. It is also important to remember that just because it is written on a page does not mean you have to use everything that is offered. Most curricula offer more than can actually be covered in one session. This is not intended to be confusing, rather to provide options. As adults, we can engage in great conversations. Part of learning for adolescents does come through activities and games. You may be tempted to drop these in the name of getting to what is really important. Know your group. Listen to what connects with them. For some students, learning comes through more active or kinesthetic approaches. Keep this in mind as you are adapting your curriculum and lessons for your youth.

As much as possible, if not you, have an adult present with your youth. It can be tempting with all of this great curriculum and the knowledge that teenagers can lead to leave them on their own. Adolescents have all the information in the world at their fingertips. The ease of the Internet, cable TV, and ever-increasing technology give them unprecedented access. What most teenagers are lacking is the guidance of wise voices to discern how to deal with all of this information. There is no substitute for an adult who is involved in their lives. You or your leaders may be intimidated by all that they know. You, however, are the adult and God has given something more than information to you. You have life experience that cannot come with any amount of study. It comes simply through living. For this reason alone, an adult needs to be present with your youth. If you or the adult volunteer either cannot pull off or simply detest the active part of learning, partner with your youth. You do not need to be the one leading the activity but do be present. When it comes time to wrestle with how this activity relates and what the lesson is for that day, your voice of wisdom is priceless.

## Youth as Part of the Total Faith Community

Some churches incorporate youth into adult classes. Your youth may attend with their parents or some other youth-friendly group of adults. Before the guilt sets in, realize that you are not alone. In fact many churches do not have specialized youth Sunday schools or bible studies. For centuries, this was the norm. As adults gathered for church, children and adolescents were considered just as much a part of the group. Youth ministry as it exists today is relatively new. For that matter, adolescents as they exist today have also changed from previous generations. If you believe that it is best to continue to have your students mixed with adult classes, do so intentionally, not by default. Talk with the leaders of those classes and with your youth to be certain they indeed belong.

Being a part of the larger church body is wonderful for youth. What is not wonderful is when youth are never given space to be the age that they are. If you are choosing to combine your teenagers with the adults, offer another time that is specific to them. Small groups, weekly discipleship, a monthly time of hanging out and talking about God in their world, looking at short series that change monthly, finding an ongoing service project, concerts, retreats, joining a neighboring church for a special event—the list goes on and on. Talk with the youth you do have. Ask them what they would like, and listen! Sometimes the thought of an ongoing group feels like more than they can do. A commitment for five weeks, however, is doable. Five-week emphases are great! One of the most beautiful things about these is that just about anyone can commit to five weeks. And once the five weeks are over, you can have a different five-week series, which makes ten weeks. After ten, add another five and you are at fifteen. Are you seeing the pattern? Build this one step at a time. Some groups will do better by being authentically involved in one another's lives and having a formal meeting once a month. If this works for you, great! If your youth decide a weekly breakfast is the best way to connect, go for it! (I know it sounds crazy, but there are lots of groups all over the country who meet before school and work on a regular basis.) Key to any choice is involving your youth. As much as possible, be the guide, not the dictator. The more they plan, the more likely they are to show up. When word gets out that an adult is actually listening, that an adult takes them seriously, others too will want to be a part of the community. A city on a hill cannot be hidden!

Teenagers do have special needs. It is important to recognize this and give a time and place to address these differences. They are wrestling with identity formation, changing bodies, and changing minds all within the context of what can be a frightening and unstable world. Psychologist Erik Erickson calls this stage of life *identity versus identity confusion*. Do you remember trying to figure out just who you were and what you believed? We all know they are growing and that changes are occurring within their bodies and hormones, but changes are equally occurring in their cognitive development. Work with your youth and create a plan that will allow space for growth and exploration in this area as well. Let your youth come up with topics to be covered. Listen. You of course know some areas that must be covered, but they know where they are questioning or struggling. Without guidance, many youth will not see the connections between their lives and God. God is not distant and irrelevant in your life, neither should God be in theirs. It is your privilege to partner with your students and find ways to build bridges between God and them. This can come during short-term classes, retreats, camp, or other special events.

## Speaking of Events . . .

Events can and will happen naturally. Be a guide; be a resource person; offer guidance; but as much as possible, let your youth plan the event. Even if you have three in your group, let those three plan a parents' night out or a family dinner and game night or a trip to the movies or whatever they dream. Not every event needs to be the equivalent of a New Year's Day parade; less is more. I can't tell you the number of pastors and leaders I have known who knock themselves out trying to wow their youth only to have no one show up. Although this feels awful, it can be more awkward when you have one or two students show up out of pity. You are embarrassed and they are embarrassed at seeing you embarrassed. Let your official or unofficial youth council take ownership. They may need help brainstorming, but ultimately let them be in charge.

Students are amazingly creative! Make dinner, get a dry erase board, and facilitate a youth group calendar brainstorming session. Brainstorming can be done several ways. Often if you ask a group for answers or ideas, everyone looks away in silence. Brainstorming is designed to get people thinking and talking. Knowing that some youth simply do not like to talk in groups, be prepared for a different way for them to express themselves. Give each person three slips of paper on which they must write at least one idea per paper. Don't forget to have paper and pencils ready ahead of time! Not only does it save the hassle of hunting through drawers, but it shows you actually thought about this ahead of time and care about what they think and have to offer. Tell them this is the time to go big or go home. Don't worry about whether the idea is actually possible at this stage; you are simply gathering ideas. Once each person has written three ideas, write them all on the dry erase board. Look for common themes to find out what your group values. Groupings may emerge around sporting events, service projects, or prayer. They may emerge around entirely different things than mentioned here. There is no right or wrong. Use this as a time to get to know your group and for the group to find its identity. You may also want to try this same process for what you as a group would like to accomplish in the next year—sponsor a child and learn about global issues or understand the ordinances or wrestle with how to witness in your community. Again, the possibilities are endless, and if the group comes up with the ideas, they are more likely to participate.

Here is another brainstorming technique. In one column, write down everything you as a group or individually love to do. In a second column write down everything you as a group or individually would love to do or learn. In a third column write down basic beliefs or convictions you have as a community of believers. The one caution: be certain that there is a God reason behind every choice you make. It is easy to slip into becoming a social club if this is not intentionally maintained. If they want to volunteer at a soup kitchen, push them to be able to say why. Look over your list of convictions and try to match an activity with each. If you believe God intends that we have an abundant life, how do you live this? If you believe God requires that we love others, are you doing this? If you believe the church is a way of life and not just what you do on Sunday, is this evident? Guide your students to connect every aspect of their life with their faith. This is a tough call for most adults, let alone teenagers. Interestingly enough, where they are developmentally actually makes this the perfect time to internalize this process.[1]

Give your youth freedom in planning activities. No one likes just to study every time they are together. Even Jesus balanced times of teaching with times of hanging out. If they like snowshoeing, go! Going snowshoeing, however, can simply be an activity, or it can be a reminder that God wants us to have an abundant life. A regular surfing date can be another activity, or it can be a chance to share your life with youth. Your youth may want to serve you! This is not a bad thing. Allowing youth to see you as an interdependent part of the community helps encourage them to be interdependent as well.

I met a youth pastor who had a sudden and dramatic onset of multiple sclerosis. He thought his days as pastor were over. What he discovered when losing the ability to go out and "do" things with his youth was that he gained the ability to "be" with them. They come for dinner once a week. What began with a small group faithfully visiting has turned into as many youth as can fit in his living room for food, laughter, prayer, and the presence of a great leader through whom God is doing great things. This was all youth-initiated and youth-maintained. They have so much to offer; just give them an opportunity to do so.

You are a builder. Your youth are also builders of your youth ministry. But remember, Christ is the cornerstone.

## Note

1. If you are a reader, check out *Practicing Passion: Youth and the Quest for a Passionate Church* (Grand Rapids, Mich.: Eerdmans Publishing Co., 2004) by Kenda Creasy Dean. She looks at the developmental lives of teenagers with their natural passions as they relate to the passion of Christ.

# CHAPTER 6

# YOUTH TODAY

*Do you have an MP3 player? Do you have a latest gaming systems? Do you listen to hip hop? Do you shop at PacSun or Hollister? Do you know what OxyContin is? If you answered no, you do not know the teen world.*

*Think about it. Today's teenagers do not know a world without cell phones, the Internet, reality television, rap, AIDS, high-tech video gaming, car seats, plastic surgery, Harry Potter, and much more. When they hear of the Simpsons, they do not think OJ's family or even Bart and Homer. They think Ashlee and Jessica.*

*So, how do we get to know teenagers? It is daunting.*

*At one church where I served, the youth ski trips were legendary. On my initial ski trip as youth minister, an unexpected blizzard dumped forty-six inches in twenty-four hours, snowing us in and giving us four feet of powder. Due to this anomaly, many unchurched high school students chose to spend the first weekend each January on the slopes with me and my chaperones. It was not because of my extraordinary skill as a speaker or my ability to relate to students. It was the snow, and the hope that there would be some magical recurrence of what had happened on that first trip.*

*On these trips I chose to do something against normal unwritten "Youth Ministry Rules." Youth in my group were permitted to bring portable music players and headphones, and they could bring whatever music they wanted. Why did I do this? The selfish reason was that I wanted some quiet as we headed*

to the mountains seven hours away early in the morning. The benefit was seeing what the kids listened to. I would walk up and down the aisles asking the
students if I could see their CD collections. I did not judge them. I got to know
them a little better and found out what they really listened to. And it was not
praise music.

## A Glimpse into Their World

Our youths love luxury. They have bad manners, contempt for authority; they show disrespect for their elders, and love to chatter in places of
exercise. Children are now tyrants, not the servants of their household.
They no longer rise when their elders enter the room. They contradict
their parents, chatter before company, gobble up their food, and tyrannize
their teachers.[1]

There is some controversy as to whether Socrates said this or not.
Whether this quote is fifteen hundred years old or simply fifty, it has been
passed down for decades now. That kind of longevity alone should be
enough to show that teenagers have long been viewed as strange at best.
It seems every generation has declared the next problematic. Missy was a
great teen to have in a group. Her hairstyle and color changed every two
weeks or so. During the few stretches she was letting a particularly short
cut grow, her friends all seemed to have new hairdos. She often did some
variation of black and spiky with different highlighted colors. I was
approached by one well-meaning but naive couple in the church as they
expressed concern over her playing keyboards up front and wondered how
they could be praying for this clearly troubled young woman. What they
didn't know was she was a godly teenager, an honor student with high
morals who desired to go to cosmetology school upon graduation. They
looked at her appearance and assumed the worst. They could not have
been more wrong. This chapter is not going to unlock every mystery for
all time regarding teenagers. What it will give is a glimpse into a world
that may not seem so long ago but indeed changes at a dramatic pace.
Although this is helpful, only in spending time with your youth will it
really come to life.

Teens today have more trials than any adult can imagine—terror alerts, metal detectors, and date rape drugs were not concerns in the previous generation. That said, teens are no worse—and no better—than most of us when we were their age. There are differences, but they are just that, differences. It is easy to forget what life was like at that age and to look back with our adult eyes in judgment on those just now going through it. Teenagers need advocates, both to hold them accountable and to see them for the people, for those created in the image of God, that we know them to be.

## Being a Youth Advocate

Your role in their life can be that of an advocate. In one of the truest senses, you may shepherd this amazing group. This world is full of trials and choices. It is not our job to make decisions for them, but that does not mean we cannot speak deeply into their lives. This is a fine balancing act.

One of my youth called after having been taken down to jail. Her parents were not the most involved and I was the adult voice in her life. She was caught shoplifting. Once when I was with her, she broke down crying, saying she didn't know how to say no to the friends who talked her into shoplifting so she did it poorly to ensure that she was caught. This let her save face with her friends while not actually getting away with the crime. I said very little as I sat with her. What she finally said to me was that she knew I would not approve, that I was disappointed, but that she also knew I would walk through this with her. She knew the right thing to do but made the wrong choice; she was indeed sorry and would never shoplift again. I gave one of the most eloquent and convicting speeches of my life all without saying a word. Just in case you are wondering, it has now been years since this happened and she has never been in trouble again.

Every day teens face difficult choices. When you have a place in their life, they listen! Whether to cheat on a test, to ditch school, or how to handle demanding parents, you have more influence than you can imagine, if you choose to claim it.

## Will They Ever Grow Up?

Emerging adulthood or delayed adolescence is perhaps the biggest shift in adolescent life in the last twenty years. While elements of this have been around forever, in westernized cultures, this is now the norm. Adolescence once lasted two or three years before a teenager would take on a full-time job. High school became mandatory and adolescence became a little longer. Now, developmental psychologists will place adolescence beginning roughly between age eleven through the mid-twenties. While this book will be looking primarily at junior high and high school students, this reality does have an effect on the youth with whom you work. For many of us, we hear these figures and want to fix it. This is one of those differences that needs to be accepted rather than declared as right or wrong. The reasons are complex and it is a trend that is here to stay.

## Are They Really Know-It-Alls?

Teenagers have more variety and choice than ever before. Having more information and more choices may seem like a blessing. Think of it this way: is it easier to decide between chocolate and vanilla or between fifty flavors of ice cream? Chances are, the more flavors, the longer the choice takes. It isn't impossible but it certainly takes longer. Now expand this to the rest of life. The Internet has changed all the rules for what information is available and who passes it down. The problem is, not all of that information is accurate. You have the experience and wisdom to help them sort through this stuff! If you know you are studying Moses the next week, ask each student to bring one interesting fact about Egypt, past or present. Don't make it like school: encourage them to find out what kind of food is liked or what do people do for fun?

It may also seem like teenagers know more than you. (Reality is they just may in some areas! And if they don't know it, they know where to find it faster than you ever could!) Knowing information and knowing what to do with it are two different things. Knowledge may be power, but a little unbridled knowledge is power out of control. You have the ability to help youth learn how to think, to discern rather than just to collect facts.

## It's a Small, Small World

Our world is shrinking. What once seemed far away is now on our nightly news, the subject of movies, and studied in Sunday school. Teenagers are interested in this world. There are questions about human rights, trade, diplomacy, and, yes, even missions. Organizations such as World Vision and Compassion International bring the suffering of children to nearly every church-related conference and even to late-night and Saturday morning television. Talk with your students about the world. But don't make this a heart-wrenching experience every time. Ask simple questions to bring in the global perspective:

- Where would you visit if you could?
- Why?
- What is the last foreign country you heard mentioned in the news or a movie?
- What do you think teenagers from other countries are doing right now? (name the country)
- What scares you for what is happening in the world?

## Just Look at the Cover of Their Magazines

Some things simply have not changed at all. They are still interested in one another, particularly what it means to be have a boyfriend or girlfriend. Interestingly, they talk very little of what it means to *be* a boyfriend or girlfriend. They are self-focused in that all the world revolves around them, but they certainly do not want to be alone. Discussions of friendship, dating, and even sex continue to be hot topics. Some of your youth will naturally be in relationships. For others, this will be a source of heartache throughout their junior high and high school careers.

Although you must talk about dating and sex, don't forget to talk about relationships in general, friendships, how you dress, and most important, finding your identity in Christ and not in someone or something else.

## Sex and Youth Culture

Sex has been and continues to be a part of the lives of youth. They are going to talk about it whether you mention it or not. Create a community in which these things can be discussed. It may take a bit of practice and prayer on your part not to look shocked at some of the questions that will come out of their mouths. This is actually a gift and a testament to their being comfortable enough with you; or it could be a test to see if you will bolt! With the spiritual and emotional damage that can be done at stake, not to mention STDs and pregnancy, talking about sex and dating is a necessity. But a word of caution: involve or at least notify the parents when you plan to discuss sensitive issues such as these. Times haven't changed that much.

## Benjamins, Bling Bling, and the New Thought of Who's Paying for What

It is no secret that the economy continues to be a point of concern. The American Dream has long been the mantra that if you work hard, you will succeed. The news has been filled with the controversy surrounding social security and what will or will not be available as today's young people hit retirement. It is even said with some regularity that the projections for this generation, for the first time in U.S. history, bring news that they will fare no better and possibly worse than their parents. Youth are aware of what is being said all around them. Issues of money have become taboo for so many. The idea of delayed gratification is almost obsolete. With the bleak outlook on the future coupled with a sense of entitlement in the present, money and materialism are consuming thoughts. Teenagers by nature are more focused in the present moment in very ego-

centric ways than mature adults are. Believing that you will fare no better than your parents can drive some teenagers to give up all hope and
simply live for the moment despite the consequences. Hope is not found
in possessions, in the present or the future. Hope is found in Christ alone.

## Pull Out Your #2 Pencil

Do you remember the anxiety? Most of us grew up with some form of
a test to tell where we stood in comparison to others. We all know the
discussions surrounding the fairness of testing; some students simply test
better than others. With the No Child Left Behind Act and increased
standardized testing, youth are constantly being measured. Depending
on the community in which you live, this can have a major effect on
your group. Some communities seem to breed high levels of anxiety over
these tests. Some communities see so little value in education that
students are sabotaged before they even begin. Some of your students
simply will not test well and will get labeled as being less than the fifti-
eth percentile.

Be aware of when testing times are coming near. Talk with your youth
about the pressures to succeed. For some of your youth, you may need to
remind them to not judge others who do not test as well. For others, you
may need to remind them that a low test score does not mean they are
not valuable. All of your youth are precious, valuable, and made in the
image of God, regardless of what those little bubble-in forms say.

## Adult Abandonment

Have you ever been to a little league game, Easter egg hunt, or church
softball game and seen "that parent" who is more competitive than any
child on the field? That is the perfect illustration of adult abandonment.
In some ways, kids have more adults present than ever before. The problem is, when they are present, it is not about the child, but about the
adult. By the time youth reach junior high or high school, adults don't

even pretend to be interested anymore. Although parents continue to be the greatest influence in the life of a child, they cannot do it alone.

Parents cannot raise their children alone. It does take a village or a community, especially if many of the parents are single for whatever reason. Other adults are needed. But often youth do not have adults interested in them. Adults come with an agenda, with a program, even though they may have the best of intentions. That's why listening is so important. Imagine coming to your youth simply to listen, to be that adult in their life who shows interest and slows down long enough just to spend time with them. It is priceless.

The Search Institute is a nonprofit organization that looks at what makes youth healthy. The Institute has a document entitled *40 Developmental Assets,* which gives the positive experiences and personal qualities that young people need to grow up healthy, caring, and responsible. Many of these positive experiences come from the involvement with adults, including coaches, teachers, and clergy. Not only are teenagers saying they want adults in their lives, but also the research shows that as well. For more information, see the web site for the Search Institute at http://www.search-institute.org.

## Come to the Altar

You don't have to look hard to see how prevalent spirituality is in this world. Music, TV, movies, books, and a whole host of other items have spirituality at the forefront of discussion. Youth are interested not just in God but in religion as well.[2] The National Study of Religion and Youth was funded by the Lilly Endowment. It has been the most comprehensive look at religion and teenagers in the U.S. to date.

An interest in religion is good news! Youth are not, as some have reported, against corporate expressions of faith. That said, if we as Christians are not paying attention to youth, if we are not making an effort to talk with them about what it means to follow Jesus and to follow him with a community, *someone else will.* Don't be afraid to be the pastor! Talk with your youth about God and church and community and coming together. The study absolutely expresses an interest and an open-ness of teenagers to religion. The problem is that they really struggle with what exactly they believe and what this means. They have a lot of information but still need adults to come alongside them to interpret with wisdom.

## An Incomplete List

By no means is this a comprehensive look at adolescents today. What it offers is a manageable snapshot. There is much more that can be said, and you can add your own insights from hanging out with the youth in your area. They are not as scary and different as they may seem at first. Despite our own insecurities, youth do want adults in their lives. You can be that adult!

A little research goes a long way. Check out a magazine; read a news-paper; watch your youth's favorite TV shows. All of these can offer peeks through the windows into the adolescent world. Another great place for research is the Internet. One of the most accessible sites is from the Center for Parent and Youth Understanding at www.cpyu.org. It is a great web site to check out for trends and news in the lives of adolescents. They will even send a regular update so that you don't have to remember to look it up! This site covers adolescent develop-ment, media, education, pop culture, sports, and more information than you could ever imagine. It's a quick way to keep up without feeling overwhelmed.

## Conclusion

Teenagers need you and the church needs teenagers. We are a family. They are important. They are not adults; don't expect them to act like adults. Neither are they children. It is a wonderful time of transition. The good news is that you can and should be a part of this change.

# Notes

1. August Kerber, *Quotable Quotes on Education* (Detroit: Wayne State University Press, 1968), 265.

2. Christian Smith and Melinda Lundquist Denton, *Soul Searching: The Religious and Spiritual Lives of American Teenagers* (New York: Oxford University Press, 2005). This is a book written from the data collected by the National Study of Youth and Religion, a four-year look at teenagers and a variety of issues. It has been much anticipated by those who work with adolescents.

CHAPTER 7

# GO WHERE I SEND YOU—AND I AM SENDING YOU WHERE THEY ARE

*While I was a youth minister, I realized I was disconnected from our middle school boys. To be honest, I was not interested in much of the things they talked about, but I decided I needed to get to know these kids (on their terms).*

*On a youth trip, I noticed the T-shirts many of them had on. They were all related to professional wrestling, something I had worked diligently to avoid since childhood. Instead of writing it off as "youth behavior," I tried a simple experiment. I asked a couple of young men about pro wrestling. Suddenly I was a friend. I was interested in them. And, they told me everything: the heroes, the villains, the intricate plots, and soap opera-like storylines. I now knew that the Sting of their world was a wrestler, not a singer.*

*During the weekend, and afterwards, I was quizzed about Steve Austin (I thought he was the Six Million Dollar Man), the Undertaker, Vince McMahon, and The Rock. I was invited to watch a match and became friends with these guys. Needless to say, I never grew in my appreciation for the complexity of the* "sport." But these young men grew in their appreciation for me as a friend and minister.

Entering their world just a little bit did not hurt my witness and did not destroy my credibility. It enhanced it in the same way it did when I visited students at the mall and at work, when I went to a concert with students, or came to a high school soccer match or even embarrassed myself at Play Station or basketball.

## The Great Commission Includes Teenagers

We may hate to admit it but most of us read the Great Commission selectively. We choose which part of the world God calls us to while enjoying the fact that missionaries *really* feel the call to go to the *really* hard places. We'll pray, send money, and praise God that we are not them! The last chapter went to great pains talking about the youth in your church, building relationships, and involving them in a variety of ways. The thought of trying to reach anyone new may be overwhelming! You already know how stretched and tired you are. This chapter will look not just at the youth in your church but the youth who, without you, may never enter your church or, worse, the Kingdom. But don't forget the chapter on volunteers! As the pastor you are the catalyst, not a solo worker.

Now here's the hard part: you don't get to choose the teenagers you want. In fact, teenagers who are easy to like and have it together are often already involved elsewhere. There are millions of youth longing for the presence of an adult in their life. They may not be able to articulate it and they may not even know that is what is missing, but we have been created to be in community. We were created to learn from those who came before us and to pass on to those who come after. We currently live in a world, as you know, where teens have access to every kind of information and entertainment imaginable. What they do not have is someone to help them with discernment, to apprentice them, to mentor them. Begin praying about where in your community God has children who are not getting the life-on-life contact God intended. Which group of youth are largely ignored or abandoned? Pray for them and pray that God opens doors for relationships that you may shepherd in places you never dreamed.

For a few years my routine included fifteen minutes twice a week at a Lebanese restaurant in Birmingham, Alabama. I had a handful of youth I knew would hang out at this place. I also learned they like being there late, just before curfew. I made a habit of getting a late-night snack or soda on the way home just so I could stop by. Inevitably I would see one or two of my youth but I would see another twenty and meet at least five while talking with my teen. I worked to not be invasive but to be friendly. Once in awhile I would sit down for long conversations, but most of the time I was in and out in just a few minutes. I became a familiar face for youth who would never have thought they would know a youth pastor. While not all of them ended up coming to church, many of them did. Interestingly, some were not at a point where they were ready to come to the group, but they found out who I was and where I served and I started receiving phone calls for one-on-one times with life-altering questions.

Oh, and by the way, I had no idea what Lebanese food was before this. I just took my cues not from what I naturally liked but from where I knew my teens were hanging out with groups of their friends. Some settings are easier than others but remember, it is not about your interest or your comfort but about going where youth are. God stepped out of the comfort of heaven to walk on this earth. We are to follow God's example and be an imitator of Christ.

## Sharing Christ

Here is the big difference in this shift of focus. No longer are you looking only at how to nurture those who come to you, but now you are looking at being intentional to share Christ with those who do not come. You must go where youth are. You can make many great contacts just by being a good pastor for the youth for whom you already have responsibilities. If your youth work, find out where and drop by once in awhile. If they are a part of a sports team, go to a game. If they are in the band or drama, go to the performance. A word of caution: don't play favorites. If you have youth in different schools, be sure you visit each. Those are the easy ones. Many of your students will not be involved in any of these. Take them on errands with you. Just hang out. Run them on their errands. Grocery shopping, washing your car or their car, or making copies are all great ways to spend a few moments together. Don't feel like you need to entertain them every time you are together. Most of life isn't entertainment. Teenagers spend hours together doing absolutely nothing.

## Fifteen Ways to Spend Time with Your Youth

(1) Drop by their work for a quick hello.

(2) Volunteer as chaplain for a sports team.

(3) Tutor once a week after school for an hour.

(4) Go to their campus for lunch.

(5) Be an assistant coach for a team.

(6) Join the band boosters.

(7) Volunteer once a week at the community center.

(8) Offer to run your teens on an errand.

(9) Go see the latest teen movie. Chances are you will see someone you know and if not, you have a new point of entry for conversation when you do.

(10) Go to the mall. Youth hang out here for hours and hours doing nothing. Again, chances are you will run into someone you know and get to know their friends.

(11) Take up a sport for your own health, but choose one you know your youth play—tennis, racquetball, basketball. Ask them to teach you.

(12) Ask around where the local hang-out is and go there to get a coffee or ice cream or whatever it is they serve.

(13) Build relationships with those who serve you at restaurants, the grocery, or your local coffee shop; often these are teenagers.

(14) Check with your city council if there is a youth task force or committee on which you may serve.

(15) Connect with a parachurch organization in your area offering to partner and be a welcoming church home.

# Parachurch Organizations

This last suggestion needs a bit of special attention. Parachurch organizations include Young Life, Youth for Christ, Campus Crusade, InterVarsity, Fellowship of Christian Athletes, and a variety of other smaller local groups. Any of the ones mentioned are reputable and looking for churches with which to partner. While each is nuanced, they all share in common reaching out to teens, sharing Jesus, and ideally connecting them with local churches. The struggle is that many churches see these organizations as a threat or are not interested in a cooperative effort.

Most of these organizations build relationships with non-churched teens. This means that if they come to you, they may still resemble the world. This can create some tension for the church, but remember, they need a different model and until you offer this, you cannot expect them to behave any differently. In other words, you will need to be intentional to set your church up as a welcoming place for the lives of teens who do not have a history with Christian values and ways of life. It is a tremendous opportunity and a great privilege. Talk with the local leaders to ask how you can best partner. They can be one of your greatest assets in building relationships with students you never would have met. You can find contact information for any of these on the web.

As you get to know representatives of these groups and as they get to know you, this will get easier. This also allows you to enter their world. There are thousands of teenagers out there who have no adult who is simply interested in them. Teenagers can tell when your motives aren't in the right place. They can tell when they are being played. Get to know your youth; get to know their friends and meet new teenagers who are not connected anywhere. You'll be amazed at the relationships God builds. It is possible that tragedy will open the door for you in the lives of teenagers as well. A youth may not come to your church but if you have taken the time to get to know him a bit, to know his name and say hello at the mall or games or wherever, that youth will seek you out when tragedy strikes.

A divorce, the death of a grandparent, or struggles with understanding war in our world are all things teenagers deal with on a regular basis.

Many have no one to help. As you have entered their world, you may not feel like you are making a difference but you are opening doors you don't realize. God does not call you to be successful; God calls you to be faithful. Be faithful in recognizing even the least of these.

## Glimpsing into Your World

As you are getting to know your youth, invite them to take a peek inside your world. While you have been called to shepherd this community, you are not the dictator. You must listen first. You listen to God; you listen to your elders; you listen to your congregation and the community. (Remember, teenagers, while young, are part of your congregation!) Simply pointing out to youth what you do goes a long way in modeling for them, not to mention establishing or building on the relationships you desire. Tell them about the responsibilities you have. Ask them what they would do if they were in the same situation. Let them become a part of your world just as you are seeking to be a part of theirs. You might be surprised to find a student who actually likes hospital visits or is skilled in thinking through logistics for the upcoming associational luncheon. This is just the beginning. While you have much to offer them, they likewise have much to offer you and your church.

## Faithfulness and Loyalty

Incarnational ministry is a way of life. It is truly sharing your life with others around you. While I would say all people benefit from this, youth in particular require it. They are still developmentally self-focused. Regardless of how great you are or how wonderful the party or concert you have planned, if they do not know you and have a relationship with you, they will not come. Once the relationship is built, you will be surprised just how loyal youth can be!

# CHAPTER 8

# JUST BECAUSE YOU WERE ONE ONCE DOESN'T MEAN YOU KNOW HOW TO TALK TO THEM NOW

*I tend to be equally forgiving and judgmental when it comes to speakers. I know how hard it can be and in that sense I am sympathetic. I also know how painful it can be to listen to some speakers. Once in awhile someone is so off in their expression of theology that I want to raise my hand in the middle and just say no . . . stop . . . can you clarify that heretical point? This happens much less often than my hurting for the well-intentioned but painfully boring speaker. Don't even get me started on those who ramble for forty-five minutes, clearly forgetting points, and by the end I have no idea what they were trying to say at all!*

*I learned a lesson just a few months ago. I was at a large conference with my small group of youth. The speaker for the evening was a very well-known speaker nationally and clearly the big name for the entire conference. Interestingly, one of my students had been in a breakout session with him earlier that day and was able to talk with him. Unfortunately, this speaker told my student he needed to get going as he was speaking that night and had no idea what passage he was using, let alone what he was going to say. Consequently, I was already annoyed at the beginning of his talk. And the talk . . . it was indeed painful. I could hardly believe this was the big name for the conference. He rambled, he was disorganized, and half-way through he said he knew he was doing a poor job and hoped that we would not judge him as it really wasn't about whether he could deliver a good message but whether the message he was delivering was good. I was torn between feeling manipulated and convicted. I was relieved when the end came. I was shocked when my students said how they appreciated his transparency and loved his points despite the poor delivery.*

## A Tale of Two Styles of Communication

It is remarkable! You can speak to the entire church every Sunday morning, be with a family at the hospital as a loved one dies, mediate conflict, cast vision, comprehend difficult theological concepts and why they are important in the world today and yet, ten minutes with a fourteen-year-old can feel more like a sentence to eternal awkwardness. Fear not, many, if not most, teenagers feel just as awkward as you in trying to know what to say.

There was a man at the church where I was on staff who was just clueless but had a huge heart! Consistently he would throw open the door of the youth room and interrupt. (Most often these came in the middle of times when an actual point was being made or we were in the midst of a deep conversation.) His interruptions were consistent! He would throw the door open with no regard for who was talking or what was going on in the room, bang on a table or the frame of the door with his cane to get everyone's attention, tell a joke, and say, "You know I love each and every one of you and I pray for you, don't you?" After a few half-hearted responses, he would leave. Every week, like clockwork, a hello-a joke-and I love you! Not a whole lot of training or even sensitivity was ever evident. He did, however, know their names and if you were new, he'd find out yours. What was amazing was the week he did not show up. When the end of the night came and we had not been interrupted it wasn't me who noticed, it was my youth. They were concerned; they missed his relentless consistency. It turned out that he had had a heart attack and was in the hospital. My youth, even the rowdiest and seemingly least caring, were touched and they initiated a time to pray for him. A couple of the youth made cards for the group to sign and took them to the hospital the next day. This man had done everything wrong when it comes to relating to students and had won their hearts!

At this same church was another man I inherited as a volunteer. He was well respected in the church community and quite a polished communicator. What I soon learned was that he was only interested in a certain few. I had a desperate need for a male junior high leader. Regardless of how sweetly he came across and how much I emphasized a great need in junior high, he simply ignored me. He would come in just before Sunday school and invite a handful of select students to his class. It made for many awkward conversations, the least of which were with the seniors who noticed he intentionally left them out of the invitation. Of course it was no better for the ones who had been singled out. While flattered at first, they felt trapped. Even worse, he never let them talk. He could communicate all right but he never listened. Consequently, what he taught most often missed the mark for what was happening in their lives. He had the prestige and technical skills but lacked humility.

## Being Real

Somewhere between these two men lies priceless insight into communicating with teenagers. Interestingly enough, they are roughly the same principles for becoming an effective communicator in any setting. The first skill is being authentic, being real. Youth don't need a show or someone cool. Adolescents are surrounded all of the time by what they think is cool, by what the media tells them is cool, and peers who may come across as cool but are, in reality, only bundles of insecurity. Every once in awhile you may have a youth who is distant, who really does come across as if he doesn't care at all about what the world thinks, let alone you.

Again, I say be yourself. Teenagers have an uncanny ability of being able to tell when you are trying to play them. You may have the best intentions in the world! Your only point may be to share the love of Christ with them. Your desire may be that they too could know of the wildly life-changing experience of following Jesus. If you are only looking to convert teens and not walk alongside them in relationship, your communication will reflect this. Even more, they will leave. If they do not or cannot physically leave, they will leave mentally.

Being authentic requires a checkup of your heart. Ask yourself, Why do I want to invest in the lives of teens? Is it because you see them as Christ sees them, created in his image and passionately wanting to be in relationship with them? Or is it guilt that is currently motivating you, guilt that you are supposed to care so you are hoping your attitude (your heart) catches up with your acts of obedience? Are pragmatics motivating you?

Even with the best people in your church, strong leadership, and a giving community, the reality is that those adults simply will not be with you forever. Investing in the lives of teenagers often falls under conversations of investing in the church of the future. So what does that say for the role of youth in the church today? If your reason for investing in teenagers is to ensure that you will have a paying job in ten years when they are in early adulthood, I will guarantee the majority of those teenagers will not be around to support you anyway! Many theologians and philosophers over the centuries have warned of this very thing . . . well, maybe not in direct reference to teenagers but certainly to the motivation behind relationships. Immanuel Kant and Dietrich Bonhoeffer each discuss making choices, in particular, relational choices, because they are the right things to do, not motivated by the potential consequence or outcomes, positive or negative. The thought is that we ought to be motivated to have a relationship with others solely based on who they are and not to get them to do something for us. All of this is to say, teenagers will know if you are talking to them to use them or if you are talking to them simply because you want to get to know them and build a relationship.

## Speak in Your Own Language

Building a relationship with teenagers also requires allowing them to know you, the real you. This can manifest in many ways and almost all revolve around communicating. The first rule, and one that should bring great relief, is don't try to talk like your youth! Language changes all of the time. There was a time when slang seemed to at least be generational. Now it changes yearly and even at times by region! Cool, hot, phat, tight, off the chain—they all mean the same thing. That's a lot of words, phrases, and meanings! The trick is to use this to your advantage, not as an overwhelming barrier or a false way of relating. Ask your youth what some of their phrases mean. This question can lead to a wonderful discussion of Scripture and language that is rich in meaning but can sometimes be confusing! Just as you don't have to talk in biblical language to be able to hear God in it, you don't have to talk like a fifteen-year-old for them to hear you. If you don't naturally talk this way, then don't (unless you are looking for a room full of laughter and eyes rolling)! When you ask what these phrases mean, you are using language to enter their world. You are communicating that they have something to teach you, that they are valuable not as they conform to your adult world but right where they are.

The flip side of this is to not talk over their heads. It's OK to teach words and phrases, but don't let time together become a vocabulary or grammar lesson. Work at not using jargon that will cause their eyes to glaze over. Remember, you are the adult here; it would be nice if they would ask you what some of your words mean but chances are they won't. Instead they will politely nod, shake their heads once in awhile, and be totally checked out from what you are discussing, unable to engage. Eventually, if they have any say about it, they will stop showing up.

## Let Your Body Language Say You Are Present

Now that you have the language fears set aside, we need to address communication in some of its other forms. Body language, facial expressions, tone of voice, and, yes, even the way you dress all send messages.

Paying attention to these will take you far. Be certain your body language does not communicate a desire to be somewhere else. If you are talking with your youth at church, don't be looking over their heads or around while in conversation with them. You may desperately need to catch one of your members before the parking lot empties, but if you are in a conversation with a thirteen-year-old, you need to be fully present with that student.

Chances are your life is extremely busy. Teenagers may not be self-aware enough to check with you before they barge in and want to talk. Consider yourself blessed if they trust you enough to interrupt your life. This is a big deal! Don't blow it by always looking busy and being annoyed when they have come to you. When sitting and talking with a group, keep your posture relaxed, not sitting back with arms crossed in judgment. Sit, enjoy, listen, and you may just be surprised at how blessed you are to be in the middle of relationships unfolding.

Teenagers will say just about anything. It is not unusual for them to say things simply to shock you. While this can be in fun, there are times when they will be sharing something real and personal for themselves as well. You may need to remind yourself of this to keep your facial expressions in check. When leading a Bible study for junior high kids, you might ask what is the most painful experience they have ever had. The answers will range from Juan's pet turtle dying to Mollie's breaking up with her most recent crush. Both are valid and hurt. If you laugh or reveal on your face that these are silly or trite, you have just lost credibility with these youth. If, however, you show that you are listening without putting them down or acting shocked, you will earn their respect.

The most difficult times will come when a student confides in you out of the blue. Just because they are young does not mean they are not experiencing some pretty horrific things. Listen with an open and nonjudgmental heart. Equally as important, train yourself to have your facial and body language to match. Just be fully present as Christ is fully present with us.

## What's on the Outside Does Matter . . . Some

It is what is on the inside that matters most. While this is true, we still make impressions based on the outside. What we wear matters. When I was growing up I always knew when we had guests. My youth pastor had "that" outfit. Without fail, he wore it and it was the signature look that stated he was cool, that he knew what young people were wearing. The problem was that we actually recognized this outfit. I also have a friend who currently is a well-known speaker in youth ministry circles. At one of those big conferences, he was speaking with a few other leaders. I noticed his particularly hip-looking outfit and of course had to point out that I guessed his son had taken him shopping. He laughed, and then said I was right. Even some of the big names in youth ministry are concerned with what they look like. You don't need to be paranoid. You do need to pay attention to what you are wearing. There needs to be a middle ground between being so adult that you show up in a suit and trying so hard that you spend a lot of cash trying to dress just like them. Find your style, casual, comfortable, clean, and put together. As one of my friends says, wearing dirty jeans and a t-shirt does not mean you can relate. On Sundays, of course you will be more dressed up, that is if you pastor a church that is dressy. The rest of the time, take cues from your youth for how casual or not, but you don't need to dress like them. They will notice if you dramatically change and it will become a joke. You are not in high school. Enjoy that you no longer need to compete in all of those unspoken ways. The more you relax in your own skin, the better you will be able to relate, and the more you will communicate to youth that they can be relaxed in their own skin too.

## Sharing Your Story

Relating is what talking with students is all about. You've got a lot to learn about them. You already know that. Have you ever thought how much they have to learn about you? Granted, this does not need to become your own personal therapy session or soapbox, but sharing your life authentically is communication.

We are a narrative society, meaning we like to tell stories. A desire in speaking with youth is finding stories that really connect. A big temptation is seeking stories that are culturally relevant and that *totally* connect. Realistically, what is culturally relevant for one student will miss the mark with another. Even in a small youth group chances are they like different kinds of music, movies, sports, hobbies, and activities. Tell stories from your own life. Even the mundane details of your life can be an illustration. Using your own stories is infinitely better than going to the many illustrations you can find online. Unless you really are reading the biography of Winston Churchill, don't quote a story from his life. Unless you really are skilled in the outdoors, don't tell a story about finding your way with a compass. If you are really bad at fixing your car, use this. If you have skills in rock climbing or are an amateur chef . . . use those things! Celebrate life and share it with your youth.

Use what is real to you. When the illustrations are real to you, you become real to your students. It will also be amazing how you get to know your students as you become vulnerable and allow them to know you.

All of these principles so far transcend both one-on-one conversations as well as group times. Telling stories and listening to stories is important. Again, balance is the key. Many leaders, in the name of being culturally relevant, give up their ministerial role and replace it with a mentorship between teenager and adult. While this is not bad in and of itself, it becomes wrong for the minister when it replaces the central role of Christ. For all Christians, not just youth workers, conversations centered on Jesus should be normative. How Jesus impacts school and family, life and choices is simply a part of the air we breathe. Modeling this kind of focus is irreplaceable. Saying the name of Jesus should not be awkward or a distinct break from daily conversations to the church ones. Jesus is not a sidebar to our lives.

> Jesus is not a sidebar to our lives.

## Want to Connect? Listen

One-on-one conversations are often considered to be the most problematic for those not accustomed to teenagers. It is amazing; you can practice open-ended questions, create brilliant opening lines, and prepare yourself for deep meaningful conversations only to find one-word responses and blank stares in return. Do not give up! Teenagers need adults in their lives. Most youth are accustomed to adults not really interested in listening to them, and they have learned how to survive these obligatory niceties. Keep trying! Listen to what they do share and remember! As you get to know them, you can ask specific questions about their lives and friends and interests. The more you listen, the more you are able to find points of connection. It is important to know that you can never underestimate the power of those short, seemingly insignificant conversations. God can and will use your efforts in tremendous ways. It may take longer than you would like and they may seem less significant than you would prefer but as the adult, it is incumbent upon you to keep trying.

## Group Topics

What to talk about in a group is another matter. Choosing what to discuss will vary greatly from group to group. There are, however, some standard topics. It may be that your church has decided upon a curriculum and many of these decisions are already moot points. But just in case, think of the following considerations. Contrary to much advice offered today, I recommend a connection with the broader church calendar. Teach about Advent and Holy Week, teach about Epiphany and the birth of Christ. I am amazed now as I meet college students from all over the country, that they are lost for several years because they recognize so little of the Christian faith apart from their home church. Offering a connection with the worldwide community of Christians is not betraying your tradition; it is grounding your youth in a way that enables them to find community with followers of Christ if they happen to leave your community.

Once church calendar events have been worked into your teaching, consider distinctives of your tradition. How do you understand salvation, baptism, the Lord's Supper, justice issues, leadership, and other important doctrines that impact belief and life? It is OK to not discuss music every week in the name of being relevant. If students are coming to a Bible study, they expect to talk about God. Even if they can't say it as junior high and high school students, they want and need to learn about their faith.

Even with teaching about the church year and tradition specific elements, you have a great deal of room to address issues that will speak to your specific group. When in doubt, ask your youth what they would like to learn. Once you have asked, listen, really listen! There are of course times when you are willing, when you are wanting to listen, only to be met with silence. This can seem like agony, but don't give up just yet. All relationships take time. Some youth will naturally be quiet or observers. Find creative ways to draw them out. You may want to take a survey asking favorite movies, songs, and Bible stories. You may include questions like: What are the top three things that worry you? What question would you ask God if you could have dinner for one night? Be creative as you put this together. After you have collected these, ask why. Another approach is to bring up a current topic from the news that week and ask how it relates to living the Christian life. One tip I have learned is that, in almost any setting, if you throw a question out to a large group, at best you will have one or two people who will respond consistently. If, however, you ask the same question, have them share their answers in groups of two or three and then have each group share, you will get much more participation. A caution: the temptation is to comment or correct every contribution the groups make. Sometimes your students will say things that are a bit off. Unless it is simply untrue or flat out harmful, let it slide. You want to encourage them to talk and wrestle with issues. Constant correction is a surefire way to shut them up.

You needn't be an expert in everything they wish to discuss. Make a list, create a plan, and do your homework. Invite them to participate with you. If they want to discuss dating (and they will), ask each of them to think about what are appropriate and inappropriate dating practices and then look at what Scripture says about relationships. If they want to discuss how to know God's will (and they will), look at a range of topics from prayer to discernment. This is an ideal time to teach on spiritual disciplines. As you create a list of topics to cover, you may need to suggest a few items along the way. Stewardship and keeping your body healthy in all ways may not be at the forefront of their minds but it will catch their interest. World events and the political climate will shape their perspective. Your part of the country as well as the economic situation will also impact understandings. As best as you can, keep these in mind as you look at topics with your youth.

Do not forget the Bible. It can become an easy pitfall to become so caught up in discussing information and relevant topics that Scripture is left behind. First and foremost when deciding what to say, when preparing for a talk, begin with Scripture and keep the focus on what God is saying to us through the Bible. It can also be too easy to assume that your youth know enough Scripture and theology to discuss their interests and lives apart from looking to Scripture again.

Outside books and extra-biblical sources can be helpful but they should never replace the Bible entirely. One of the greatest gifts that you can give to your youth in teaching and speaking is the gift of not needing to have you by their side in order to seek wisdom from God. Knowledge of the Bible keeps them grounded and takes the pressure off you to be the center of their faith.

There is no magical formula for speaking with teenagers. There are a few principles that can help you find your unique voice. As you teach your students to be who God has created them to be, your best teaching will come as you model this yourself. There are volumes on how to be a better speaker. There are tips and lists and pointers that can be found at the click of a button. (In fact I recommend checking out web sites including www.ileadyouth.com or the Youth Specialties web site, www.youthspecialties.com. Look at the archived articles under communication for several other takes on talking with teenagers.) You can always improve. While this is good and I recommend seeking out resources, do not be so caught up in needing to be good that you are paralyzed from beginning. God can and will use you, if you are willing. Be yourself, not who you were when you were a teenager, but who you are now!

# CHAPTER 9

# IF YOU TAKE NOTHING ELSE FROM THIS BOOK...

Youth ministry can feel at times like being a jack-of-all-trades and master of none. This isn't quite true but it can feel like every time you turn around that there is something else you need to know. This chapter offers a collection of wisdom, practical advice, and helpful suggestions. Youth ministry has changed a great deal in the last twenty years. What was once acceptable is no longer. This chapter will show you some nuts and bolts of today's youth ministry.

## Volunteer Etiquette

It seems this should go without saying, but there should be no dating between youth and volunteer or paid youth workers. It wasn't long ago when, while this may not have been the ideal, it was accepted or at least tolerated. Often those who volunteer will be first- or second-year college students. Realistically, they are not that much older than the high school juniors and seniors. While the age difference may not be that great, this is still a very bad idea.

Occasionally you will have two people with an even greater age differ-ence who become interested in one another. Regardless of the age issue, dating shifts the dynamics of the group considerably. There is also the issue of what happens if and when they break up. An even more grave possibil-ity is the issue of sexual abuse or statutory rape or even untrue gossip about the relationship. This is never a fun topic but it is a reality for the world in which we live. More information will be offered on this in another section.

## Background Checks

A background check needn't be a traumatic event. If this is standard operating procedure, it is simply a way of gatekeeping. Talk with your local police department and find out the easiest way to participate in this kind of system. Even if your church is small, this is a possibility. Your budget may be small but protecting your teens needs to be a top priority. Most churches work on such a relational level that taking advantage of someone becomes very easy. You should absolutely be the first to participate. Set the tone and let each potential volunteer know that it is not a personal matter, but rather each and every person will be going through this. If he or she refuses to participate, *do not* assume the worst. Some people just are not comfortable with background checks. Unfortunately, this also means that they cannot become one of your workers. A background check can also help in case there is an emergency once they are volunteers.

In regard to protecting your youth and your church, make sure that you know what your liability insurance covers. Be sure that you, as the pri-mary responsible adult, are covered under the church policy. Be sure you know what your limits of liability are in case of any incident.

## Abuse

This is not the fun part of youth ministry but it is all too common. Abuse comes in many forms: physical, sexual, emotional, verbal, spiritual, and neglect. Each of these carries with it a burden no person, let alone a teenager, should have to carry. Talk about abuse within your group: what it is, how to talk about it, who to tell. Incorporating it into talks and lessons as a normal part of the discussion lessens the stigma and shame of bringing up the topic for a victim. Remember that if you have even one hundred persons in your church, you will also have more than seven and perhaps as many as fifteen who have been or who are being abused.

I spoke for a church just a few months ago during their *True Love Waits* month. Each year they do a month-long series and one week is dedicated to better understanding God's heartache over sexual abuse, the signs it is occurring, how to recognize it, and how to find help. It may seem obvious to you what constitutes abuse but many people simply think they deserve or have caused the behavior.

Dating violence is an all-too-common occurrence among adolescents and is not acceptable. I am always shocked at the number of teens who tell me they thought this was what dating was like and accepted it. This church offered a brilliant way to inform, to plant seeds that this kind of behavior is unacceptable, and to offer practical tools to use knowing that this indeed will happen to one of your youth or one of their friends. If you are not comfortable addressing this topic, ask around your church. Do you have any social workers or counselors? Call the local police department to see what kind of education/outreach program they may have.

Other forms of abuse need to be addressed as well. There are several ways to do so. Even simply setting ground rules for how you speak to one another is a teachable moment. Ask how you know what is all in good fun and what becomes hurtful? How can teasing turn to mocking turn to abuse? Ground rules for how you play together are also helpful. Finding a curriculum that addresses abuse can be difficult. The Faith Trust Institute, www.faithtrustinstitute.org, offers a uniquely faith-based perspective addressing these major issues. They have a curriculum not just for teens but for the entire church. This is an excellent idea for prevention, intervention, and raising awareness. Be certain you have thoroughly prayed through this as chances are there will be some follow-up needed. Be ready with the phone number of a local counselor you trust. The Faith Trust Institute also offers pamphlets with hotline numbers. An easy and effective way to offer help not just for the youth group but for the church is to place these pamphlets in the restrooms. Some people will never talk about this and would never pick up a brochure on a resource table at the back of the church for fear of being seen. Offering help with discretion sends the message that not only are you concerned and taking a firm stance but that you care about what a difficult situation this can be overall.

## Referrals

Being a jack-of-all-trades and master of none does not include counseling beyond that for which you are trained. You are a pastor. Being a pastor entails specific legal rights and privileges regarding confidentiality. Make sure you know the laws in your state regarding the limits of pastor confidentiality. This can protect both you and your congregation. Consult the local police department and/or an attorney. Also know that laws change on a regular basis. There may not be dramatic changes but there will be nuances and it is in your best interest to stay abreast of these.

Being a pastor is more than a full-time job in and of itself. And youth ministry may bring with it a whole host of specific issues that may need to be addressed by persons with specific expertise. It is a good idea to have a few referrals on hand at any given time just in case. If you do not know where to begin looking, begin in your own church. Do you know any counselors or therapists? It may be that the person you know does not want to be the referral for your church because of the close personal connection, but they will know someone who is trustworthy and will not violate a Christian perspective. A word of caution: just because the person is a Christian therapist does not make him or her a good therapist. Get references. It is standard operating procedure for a therapist to offer references. If you do not have any counselors or therapists in your church there are still many options. Call your local hospital, the local middle or high school, and look on the web sites of seminaries that offer psychology, pastoral care degrees, or who may be affiliated with local counseling centers. You might get in touch with the social work or psychology department at a college nearby. State what you are wanting and most will be happy and helpful as you gather referrals.

There are many areas where you should refer. But know that you are the first line of defense. You will often be the first to learn of abuse, alcoholism, depression, and many other very serious issues in our world today. Your congregation, including teenagers, needs for you to be their pastor. You may continue to meet and pray with the person needing help but be open to not needing to do it all. Many of the best-intentioned pastors have become overwhelmed with the struggles of the people God has placed in their care. Referring is not a failure! In fact, it is one of the most loving, responsible actions you can take.

## Issues Needing Referrals

Adolescents have always faced struggles. Youth today have a whole new world of issues many of us never considered. At least be aware of the trends so that you may be able to recognize problems or at least not look shocked when a teen tells you of a deep struggle. Can you think of the issues that teens face daily? Make a quick list and see if you included any of the following:

(1) alcohol, either trying it or abusing it
(2) drugs, street and prescription
(3) dating violence, a greater incidence among adolescents than other age groups
(4) eating disorders: anorexia, bulimia, and obesity
(5) depression
(6) sexual issues: pregnancy, AIDS, other STDs
(7) abuse: physical, sexual, verbal, emotional, and spiritual
(8) pornography
(9) cutting (not ditching classes—self-mutilation)
(10) grief/bereavement
(11) suicide
(12) sexual identity issues
(13) gambling

These are just a few of the issues facing teens today. While you do have a place in their lives and you can offer the Christian perspective, you needn't be alone in this effort. In fact, you can do more damage than good if you choose to ignore your own limitations.

## Hotline Numbers

The following is a list of national hotline numbers to aid in moments of crisis. I encourage you to find your local numbers and keep them in a place you will remember, but this is a good resource as a backup.

**Suicide**
The Jason Foundation
1-800-Suicide

**Rape**
VOICES in Action:
1-800-VOICE-8

**Rape Abuse Incest National Network Hotline**
1-800-656-HOPE (656-4673)

**Abuse**
National Domestic Violence Hotline
1-800-799-SAFE (799-7233)

**Childhelp, USA**
1-800-4ACHILD (422-4453
TTY 1-800-2ACHILD (222-4453)

**Runaway/Crisis Intervention:**
National Runaway Switchboard
1-800-621-4000

**Boys Town National Hotline**
1-800-448-3000
TTY 1-800-448-1883

## Forms, Permission Slips, and All That Stuff

There was a time when you would pile into whatever vehicle was available and take off for the weekend. Those days are long gone. For off-campus trips, be certain you have a permission slip with emergency contact information on hand. In fact, this is a good thing to keep on file when at your church as well, just in case a rogue skateboard goes rolling by, rendering your teen unconscious on the ground!

You might consider keeping two files for each youth, one to keep at the church and one to take with you on trips. A few forms to keep on file would include a basic bio with current contact information for parents and/or guardians, permission slips, and medical release forms with medical insurance information, and a form listing any special needs a particular youth may have (dietary, medication, etc.) There are many other forms that can make life easier and help you to look and be more organized, but these are the main ones. An excellent comprehensive resource for finding reproducible forms and tips for ministry management is *Youth Ministry Management Tools* by Ginny Olson, Diane Elliot, and Mike Work (Grand Rapids: Zondervan, 2001). Please remember that these forms will need constant updating before trips.

Before leaving on a trip, be sure parents know who will be driving and that the drivers have their car insurance up-to-date. If you have a church van or bus, be sure you know who is licensed to drive, what insurance the church carries, and who to contact in the church to make sure the van or bus is in good working condition.

## Greatest Joys, Biggest Sorrows

I was once sent a cartoon that had Ziggy looking at the ice cream that had fallen on his foot, and the caption stated, "How is it that what was once our greatest joys become our biggest sorrows?" I think this is how much of life is. When you care deeply, you cannot help but to celebrate when your youth do well and to feel it deep in your soul when you see them fall. They can be both your greatest joy and biggest sorrow. What I wish I had been told early on was to not let this be my litmus test, what determined if I was to stay committed to teenagers or not. It has been a learning experience to accept that regardless of the emotional rollercoaster that occurs, it is the calling that determines the ministry, not the joys and sorrows.

There are a few other things I wish I had been told during the beginning of my time with teenagers. Many of these I have already mentioned throughout this book. I wish that I was told to quickly and openly say "I don't know" when I didn't. Pretending leads to confusion and a lack of trust. Admitting you have more to learn makes you approachable and real. Being the adult, even the adult pastor, does not make you infallible. Do not be an example that no one can live up to. One of the most amazing ways to encourage teens is to let them see the real you intentionally seeking to follow Jesus.

I also wish I had been told to give opportunities for students to excel but to not count on them so much that I was angry or disappointed when they (gasp) behaved like teenagers. Youth do have much to offer but they are still growing and developing. I mistook their passion for maturity and was often let down either in that they did not follow through or their interests waned quickly. Celebrate where they are when they are. Encourage consistency but do not lose hope if they shift their attention or do not pull something off as well as you would have liked.

Finally, and most importantly, allow God to minister to you through your youth. They are not Christians-in-waiting; they are not soon to be the church. They are uniquely created in the image of God and have something to offer the body of Christ now. They may not be able to articulate in the same way as an adult but it just may be when the polish is off and the crude offerings of a fourteen-year-old shine through that deep truths finally make their way to the community. Know that the acceptance of a teenager is a testament to your life. They can and will fill you with more encouragement and hope than you ever dreamed.

Any truthful youth pastor will tell you that we get something out of being with teens. If receiving benefits is the only motivation, I say find another place to serve. Being blessed by serving youth, however, is natural and normal. They are life-giving, full of energy, confusing, and dynamic all at the same time. Take this as a blessing and confirmation that you are doing something of God.

Enjoy your time with them. They will grow quickly. While you will always have teenagers, for each one, the time is short. Be a wise steward of those whom God has brought into your world. Keep them safe. Care for them. Love them as if you were loving Jesus himself. They may seem powerful and intimidating but they are still an overlooked voice, misunderstood and vulnerable. Take care of them, body and soul. Be the minister God has called you to be and see how he multiplies beyond what you could ever imagine.